Saving Samantha

A young woman's escape
from childhood hell

Samantha C. Weaver

HAY HOUSE

Australia • Canada • Hong Kong
South Africa • United Kingdom • United States

First published and distributed in the United Kingdom by:
Hay House UK Ltd, Unit B, 292 Kensal Rd, London W10 5BE.
Tel.: (44) 20 8962 1230; Fax: (44) 20 8962 1239. www.hayhouse.co.uk

Published and distributed in the United States of America by:
Hay House, Inc., PO Box 5100, Carlsbad, CA 92018-5100. Tel.: (1) 760 431 7695
or (1) 800 654 5126; Fax (1) 760 431 6948 or (1) 800 650 5115.
www.hayhouse.com

Published and distributed in Australia by:
Hay House Australia Ltd, 18/36 Ralph St, Alexandra NSW 2015.
Tel.: (61) 2 9669 4299; Fax: (61) 2 9669 4144. www.hayhouse.com.au

Published and distributed in the Republic of South Africa by:
Hay House SA (Pty) Ltd, PO Box 990, Witkoppen 2068.
Tel./Fax: (27) 11 706 6612. orders@psdprom.co.za

Distributed in Canada by:
Raincoast, 9050 Shaughnessy St, Vancouver, BC V6P 6E5.
Tel.: (1) 604 323 7100; Fax: (1) 604 323 2600

A catalogue record for this book is available from the British Library.

ISBN-10 1-4019-1030-0
ISBN-13 978-1-4019-1030-3

Printed and bound in Great Britain by TJ International, Padstow, Cornwall.

Dedicated to Geoff Hosier
(14th March 1945–23rd July 2002).
My father figure, my friend and my Guardian Angel.
A promise made and kept. I got there in the end;
I hope that I have made you proud.

ACKNOWLEDGEMENTS

A heartfelt thank you to everyone who has made this book possible. With special thanks to my GP, counsellor, therapist, psychiatrist and the entire team at the Cardinal Clinic; without your perseverance, guidance, support and understanding, I would not be here today.

Thank you to Mandy, Kieley and Scott for being there for me as a family when I needed it the most.

Thank you to Sheila, Gavin and the children for giving me my first chance to lead a normal life.

Thank you to Lesley and David for the support you have given me over the past few years.

Thank you to all of my friends who have given me the encouragement, confidence and belief in myself to write this book – you know who you are.

Thank you to the whole team at Hay House Publishing for making my wish a reality.

And finally a huge thank you to my editor, Susanna Forrest, who has skilfully transformed this book into something I could never have imagined. You have a special talent; and throughout the whole process you have been wonderful, I cannot praise you highly enough.

The little things that each of you have done for me mean more to me than you will ever realise, and because of every one of you, the completion of this book has resulted in final closure to my nightmares and pain. I can now optimistically look forward to a new chapter in my life.

Author's note

Some of the names in this book have been changed in order to respect and protect the identity of individuals. This book has been written expressly as my personal account of the events in my life and as such is my interpretation and my version of events. Under no circumstances has this manuscript been written as an opportunity to be vindictive or malicious. I sincerely hope that it will provide others with hope and inspiration for their own lives.

INTRODUCTION

Saving Samantha is my personal story of recovery from the depths of depression. I was abused, neglected, starved of love and support, by my severely disturbed and mentally unstable father and complicit mother, and this resulted in scarring me for most of my life.

All of my best efforts throughout my youth and into early adulthood to "get better" had failed me. I believed I had tried every option that was available to me to rid myself of my past, my issues and my depression, but I was wrong. I continued to leave a trail of broken relationships and friendships, which left me with only overwhelming feelings of guilt, frustration and isolation. I pushed away the people that were trying to help me, by testing them harshly and continuously, until I reached a point where I could finally take no more and had to accept help; depression had consumed my life

Leaving the psychiatric hospital where I'd been for a month-long stay because of a suicide attempt, it suddenly hit me hard that I had to use everything I had learned if I wanted to survive and be happy. I had to be determined, I had to be strong, I had to encourage myself to argue with my negative thoughts (my "chatterbox"); I had to know that I would never again experience feelings of angst, anger, sadness, isolation and depression to that extent. In hospital, I was finally given the chance to exorcise my demons and after doing so I began to believe that there was a chance for me to have some sort of happiness in my future.

Throughout this book, I explain my feelings of rejection, confusion and anger, and the ways in which I exasperated my issues in day-to-day life and again in a safe and controlled manner while hospitalised. Battling daily with depression and feelings of hate and anxiety, I explain how I attempted to protect myself day-to-day by creating and living in a fantasy world, enveloping myself within mentally constructed barriers in an attempt to protect myself from being hurt anymore.

After many long and arduous battles, I have now succeeded in beating my depression. This is my personal story of triumph and hope.

CONTENTS

CHAPTER 1

Vague but painful memories

Whenever I dare to think back to my childhood, the first thing that comes to me is my father's voice, deep and harsh: "Do as you are DAMN well told!" The thought of it still makes me wince; it was scalding – whatever my sisters or brother or I said was dismissed. We weren't allowed to answer back or have opinions or even feelings.

My parents never cuddled me, or comforted me; the words "I love you" were never spoken. We were never praised for anything; they just told us we were rude, naughty, disobedient children, whatever we did. We "had to learn the hard way" but they told us all the time that we "wouldn't amount to anything". One of my father's favourite lines was, "I was treated this way, so you kids will be treated the damn same." He'd add that it hadn't done him any harm, but looking back as an adult, I would disagree and say that was rubbish. Something must have made him the way he was, and he should never have inflicted the same on us.

His voice made my sisters and brother shrink into themselves, but I didn't want to be invisible and I tried to stand up to it. I'm sure it would have been far worse if I hadn't. I think people thought I was a confident, loud and brash child, but it was all an act I used to protect myself from that voice and everything it meant; and it always meant that I was worthless and would be punished for it.

Now when I think back and hear his voice, I know that there is nothing that could ever scare me like that again, whatever life throws at me. After all I have been through and learned I am strong, but this wasn't always the case. I've come a long way from the frightened, defiant child that I was, but it's been a tough journey, and I thought I was lost a good many times.

I grew up, fast, on a rough council estate that the local authorities didn't bother keeping nice, with my Mum and Dad, three sisters and a brother. I can still picture our house clearly: the lawn was wild, nobody ever mowed it and the grass reached as high as my waist. The upper floor of the semi had once been painted white but was now grey and peeling, the brickwork below was shabby and crumbling with neglect.

Downstairs there was a kitchen and a living room and a small bathroom, though the toilet was outside in a shed. There were three bedrooms upstairs. My parents occupied one, my little brother Jacob and my older half-sister Sarina were crammed into bunk beds in the box room, and the third was for me and my sisters Charmaine and Jocelyn. I spent most of my childhood in that bedroom. It had old, faded woodchip wallpaper and there was mould spreading from the windows, making everything smell musty. We had no carpet and my parents had bought the furniture cheaply from jumble sales or scavenged it from the tip – it was usually broken. Sometimes they even picked up the junk our neighbours had thrown out on the street and we had to make do with that.

Jocelyn was older so she had the cabin bed, while I shared a bunk bed with Charmaine – she had the bottom bunk because she was the youngest. We'd each carved out a bit of territory from the floor, where we could keep the few personal things we had. There was no central heating in the house, just a gas fire in the living room, which Mum stood us in front of in the winter when we dressed for school. As the window frames in our room were rotting our sheets were always cold and clammy. The fireplace there was never lit.

As I lay in my bunk in the winter I could see my breath rising up to the ceiling. On really cold days, Mum got round to giving us hot water bottles, but they went cold in no time at all and felt unbearable against your skin so I'd wake up and fling them to the floor.

Above the empty fireplace in the bedroom was an old white mantelpiece. Sometimes my mother would come in at night and leave us a custard cream biscuit each and a glass of milk to share for breakfast. We were always hungry, and on one or two occasions Jocelyn woke up in the middle of the night and devoured all three biscuits, and Charmaine and I went without our "breakfast". We didn't realise, and just thought Mum had run out of biscuits. Jocelyn confided in me about it years later and explained how guilty she felt. I can't eat breakfast now; which I suppose is something to do with remembering that hollow feeling of waking up starving and not being able to do a thing about it.

You might wonder why we didn't just sneak down to the kitchen to steal something to eat, but that was impossible because we were all sent to bed at 7 sharp each night and my parents would lock the door on us. That was it until morning and the three custard creams. We just weren't allowed out again, not even to go to the loo. When the lock broke because the door had been slammed, Dad just let it be known that we weren't allowed out till he said so, and that was that. At weekends my mother and father had a lie in until lunchtime, and we'd be awake, famished and restless for hours, caged in the room but desperate to make the most of a day free of school. It was no use – they never budged.

We were given a big red plastic bucket with a white handle: this was our toilet. If we used the bucket there was no paper, so we wiped ourselves on the floor or on a sock. It sounds disgusting, and it *was*, but being young and naïve we didn't know any better. I used to think all children were treated the same way. Sometimes I'd try to hold on to my bursting bladder till we were allowed up, then race to the toilet outside.

On one or two terrible occasions we knocked the bucket over while playing and were petrified. What would our father say when he found out? Desperately, we used our school shoes to scrape up the excrement as best we could and tried to hide the rest under the wardrobe. Then we dragged a chest of drawers over the wet, stinking stain. My parents never questioned the stench – they just wanted to know why we'd moved the furniture around, so we lied and said we'd just fancied a change. Anything to stop them getting angry with us.

The real toilet was in an outhouse in the garden; it had a wooden door with a broken bolt and it never quite shut properly so I was always worried that someone would break in on me. I wondered if our parents wouldn't let us use it at night because a trip outside would have meant the fuss of unlocking the back door, but when the council finally replaced it with a new indoor bathroom suite we were still locked in our room with the bucket.

Of course, it wasn't just our father's tongue that paralysed us with fear. He backed up his verbal threats with physical violence, and we never knew when we would be attacked. One thing guaranteed we'd be beaten, though, and that was talking in bed after we'd been shut into our room for the night. Absolute quiet was expected, and my dad even installed a microphone in the bedroom which was connected to a speaker in the living room so he could sit downstairs watching the telly and still hear if we were whispering.

Sometimes he'd shout upstairs that he'd come up and give us a hiding; sometimes he came straight up; and sometimes, worst of all, he wouldn't be in the living room at all but standing silently outside the bedroom door, waiting and listening. It was like he wanted to scare us, to hurt us, and was just waiting for an excuse to do it. The door would bang open and he'd step in, the light from the hall behind him. He'd unbuckle his belt and fold it once, slapping the leather together. I think he enjoyed that bit of theatre, and the sound was enough to make me tremble violently. My heart would begin to race so fast I'd think it might burst out of my chest and my stomach would churn nauseously. The thought of that sound still makes me shake – it puts me right back there in my bunk bed, a terrified little girl again.

It didn't matter who had been talking; we all got punished. I was first, because I was bigger than Jocelyn. After her came Charmaine. We'd worked out this order between us, thinking that by the time he turned to her his arms would be tired and Charmaine wouldn't be hit so hard. One by one we'd climb out of our beds and walk over to brace ourselves against the wall, placing our palms flat against it, bent over so that our bottoms were sticking out. Father would lift up our nightdresses to expose our skin and raise the hand with the belt in it high above his head. Then he'd let us have it.

When his arm lashed down I would feel shock and electricity shoot up my spine, then an awful burning on my buttocks. The pain was excruciating, but the second strike was the worst, because the first would still be stinging. By the third I was pretty much numb, it couldn't add any more pain.

Then he'd grab my arm, yank me from the wall and swing me back to my bed, yelling "Next!" and Jocelyn would have hell to pay if she kept him waiting. Charmaine would be crying already, petrified. We were all beaten so many times as children that we knew exactly what was coming from the moment the stairs creaked or the handle turned on the door. We also knew that if we didn't cry enough he would call us back to the wall, and continue to belt us till we did.

Back in bed I'd lie on my front, trying to keep the sheets off my bottom which was throbbing agonisingly. Jocelyn and Charmaine would take their beatings and crawl back into bed, sniffing and weeping, and Father would fasten his belt back on and stalk out, slamming the door. He'd yell back through the keyhole, "Shut up and go to sleep! Or I'll be back in there to give you another good hiding!"

We'd wait in silence, listening to his footsteps going back down the stairs. Then I'd risk a whisper to ask the others if they were ok. They'd always snuffle back that they were fine, and that I should shut up in case Dad heard me. We all knew that we weren't ok. By morning the welts had usually faded. There was no evidence. My mother never intervened, even if she wasn't out working a night shift, and stayed in the living room while we were thrashed black and blue. It's hard to understand how she could do this. I think she was scared of my father too, but she always took his side, and when she thought we wouldn't listen to her she would threaten us by saying "Wait till I tell your father", then let him loose on us. She had no problem with that. She was complicit in everything he did.

Jacob was never punished that way – in fact I don't remember him ever being beaten. I felt that he was both Mum and Dad's favourite; he was the baby, and Dad had wanted a son to carry on our surname because it was so unusual. I'm sure if any of us girls had been born a boy, he wouldn't have bothered having any more children.

Jacob was never locked in his room; he could get up early, have breakfast and go out to play. Being the youngest, he was always home first from school and would be settled in front of the TV with control of the remote by the time the rest of us came in. If any of us girls tried to change channels he'd punch, kick, scream and shout for our mother, and she'd give us a slap for fighting with him.

Of course, when my father came home, she'd tell him I'd been winding up Jacob – it was usually me – and I'd be punished. Jacob's box room was next door to ours, so he must have heard us being beaten, but he never said anything about it to us or to anyone else. I hated that he was treated differently, and when I was younger the only thing I could do was tease him about it – I called him "Daddy's favourite little boy" and told him he was just like Father, which was the worst thing I could think of. Even he didn't like that.

If my mother ever defended any of us girls it was Jocelyn, and naturally Jocelyn sided with her in an argument. As we grew older, this divide between us got wider, and by our teens we didn't have much common ground. I suppose it was just Jocelyn's way of dealing with the precarious situation in our house, and when she had an ally in my mother she had some defence from my father. It didn't make her independent though and only dug her deeper into our strange, messed up family.

Little Charmaine coped differently too. She was too young to work out the best way through the minefield of "good" and "bad" behaviour, which was always changing according to Dad's mood. The slightest thing sent her into hysterics. Screaming got my parents' attention, and it got right on their nerves, so very often Charmaine and I would both get a clip around the ear from Mother and then a slap from Father – me for "provoking" Charmaine, Charmaine for making such a racket. She never learned.

I was branded the "difficult, moody child" in this family of bullies and victims because I was striving to stand up for myself. I don't believe I was any more "difficult" than any other young child – I was mischievous and I rowed with my siblings, but I also believed we didn't deserve such harsh treatment, and I became more and more aware that it was wrong as I got older. I also felt like I'd been singled out for punishment when the others were excused. We didn't even have to do anything bad to be smacked. The person who decided the rules was my father, and only my father; everything had to be as he saw it or else it wouldn't be tolerated.

He was a tall, skinny man with slicked-back black hair and a pony tail which he used to twiddle into a single curl with his fingers. He had a receding hairline, a black beard and brown eyes that also turned black when he was angry. He had a tattoo on each arm: a scroll in a heart with the name Marge (my mother) in the middle, and another which said "Mum". Neither he nor Mum washed often, and he smelled stale and nasty – I still catch that smell from people with bad body odour occasionally, like pencil shavings, and I don't think I'll ever forget it. The stench of his feet was almost unbearable.

He always wore leather wrist supports and he used to tell everyone he'd once had an accident and had had an operation to fix a metal plate into his wrist bones. He was full of wild, exaggerated stories. He liked to show off the scar. He'd thought the leather strap was cool, and didn't remove it after the operation as recommended by the doctor, and then he'd got one for the other hand, claiming his arms had got dependent on them over the years, and had got too weak to go without them. Having "weak wrists" never stopped him thrashing us, strangely enough.

He also suffered very badly from migraines, which must have been excruciatingly painful. It jacked his hearing up until it was hypersensitive, so we kids could barely squeak and he'd be at our throats. If he had gone to bed during the day to weather an attack we'd try and creep about the house silently, but he'd come roaring out of his room if he heard us, yelling that he had "a fucking migraine and if I hear one more sound out of you you'll get my belt so fucking hard you won't know what's hit you!"

In the 1980s he worked as a car mechanic and had built his own garage on the side of the house where he did jobs for people he knew. I remember him working on an orange MG for months at a time. It was a wreck when he first started on it, rusty and dented with a rip in the convertible roof. By the time he was done it looked like a new car and the owner was ecstatic. As we were growing up Dad had all kinds of different old cars – a blue Jaguar, a big yellow American Yank, a stretch Dorchester Limousine, and even a hearse at one point. I hated the cars, as when we drove around the neighbourhood everyone would wave at us as if we were royalty, just because of the car, and that couldn't have been further from the truth.

My father also had lots of wild schemes and bright ideas to make us rich beyond our wildest dreams and he often swept others along in his enthusiasm. The neighbours would really believe he'd cracked the code for winning the National Lottery, or that he'd write a book and set up his own publishing company. My Mum was the first person to fall for these pointless quests, but later she got wise as none of them ever worked. She learned just to nod along with the rest of us and say nothing. Even she didn't think my father would ever make a million and, as far as I know, he still hasn't!

He had a reputation on the estate as a hard man, but I could never work out why as I don't remember him actually attacking anyone his own size. He could rage so wildly that grown men probably had second thoughts about taking him on. Perhaps that intimidated people so much they would never have thought of reporting the family to Social Services. It made him notorious in the neighbourhood. He was the chief bully in our house too, and when we were little none of us stood up to him.

My mum was his biggest supporter – maybe his only real ally. She left home at 19 to marry him, literally running off halfway through a family dinner and just about cutting herself off from my grandparents, who were baffled and devastated. My dad just appeared in a car outside their home, tooted his horn and she scarpered with a suitcase she'd had packed and ready. She agreed to take on my half-sister Sarina when Dad got custody of her, and, even after she'd had four kids of her own, she still earned most of the household's steady income. Neither she nor my dad had any qualifications, having left school at 14, so she took whatever jobs she could, working as a dinner lady, a night assistant in a care home or a lollipop lady.

She was a big woman. I've seen pictures of her in her early twenties and she was very slim then, but after having children she piled on weight quickly. My father used to point this out, and say she'd got lazy. When she wasn't about to go out to work she always wore the same shabby nightdress which was covered in all kinds of stains, from coffee to excrement. Her hair was reddish and tied back flat and greasy against her head – her skin was really oily too.

Her horn-rimmed glasses were fitted so tightly to her face that there was an indent in her nose. She only washed once a week, like the rest of the family, and stank even more than my father. She had a habit of scratching her teeth, which were yellow, to get the plaque off, but it never worked. She would sit in the living room snipping off dead skin from her dry, cracked feet with toenail clippers and sometimes she cut too deeply and drew blood.

I thought she was repulsive, and swore that I'd never end up like her. People thought I was more like my father, but obviously I didn't want to take after him any more than her! I used to daydream for hours that I wasn't their child, and that the nurses had given them the wrong baby when they left the hospital. That way, my real parents might come and rescue me one day, and I'd have a new, better life. It never happened, but I could always hope and flesh out the fantasy in my head, and that helped get me from day to day.

As a very small child you simply accept what happens in your home as "normal". For me it was "normal" to be locked in my room and told I was stupid and ugly. It was "normal" to be beaten or grounded for the smallest things. Our household had its own routine which I had become accustomed to, and as my parents seemed to isolate us deliberately from the rest of their families and from any potential friends, I didn't know any different until I was almost in my teens.

CHAPTER 2

Family life

The family was dominated by two things, a lack of money and my father's temper. Between my parents' earnings and pay outs from social services, we should have been solvent, but somehow my dad was always running up huge debts. I was told once that he'd been made bankrupt when we were very young, but I don't even know what he kept spending all the money on. People would come round to collect the debts and we'd have to hide. One minute we'd be sitting watching the telly, and the next there'd be a furious banging on the front door and Mum would fly into a panic.

She'd tug us off the sofa and hustle us under the long, brown curtains with an orange flower pattern, saying, "Shut up and don't make a sound!" A shadow would stretch over the wall above the sofa as the bailiffs peered in. We'd sit it out and eventually they'd give up and we'd hear their van pulling away. This happened about once a week. Sometimes we had the money to pay, but then it was always Mum and not Father who faced them on the doorstep. It was like living under siege, and the tense atmosphere unnerved us kids. When I left home and got a job I thought the most important thing I could do was to stay in the black, because memories of that panic were so vivid to me.

Father's idea of dealing with it was to install cameras near the front door. If someone knocked, he could flip the TV to channel 11 and see who was outside via the video camera. If it was a bailiff or someone he didn't know, he wouldn't move. If the person was "OK", one of us kids would be sent to open the door. He was twitchy about anyone who used the front door, so if we dared to have friends to visit we had to tell them to come straight round to the back of the house.

While Dad spent the money on – well, whatever it was he spent the money on – Mum was in charge of the household budget, and she scrimped every last penny she could. To save on water bills and heating she would wash us in the kitchen sink. It was cheaper to fill than a bath. She'd strip us down, place a thin tea towel on the sideboard and run a sinkful of hot water. We had to crawl one at a time off the sideboard into the sink, and she'd use a plastic beaker to sluice us with water. She used Imperial Leather soap – I still hate the smell of it – and a rough flannel that scratched our skin.

She'd really scour our necks, muttering that they looked like a "potato sack", turning them bright red. When she was done she'd plonk us back down on the tea towel and rub us with another towel, which so stiff it left our skin raw. Then it was the next child's turn in the same filthy water, on the same tea towel, which was now cold and damp. We were only bathed once a week and I got more and more self-conscious about this as I got older. Some girls at school started calling me "smelly" but I couldn't wash more often, and when I was a teenager I couldn't get hold of deodorant because Mum would never have added anything to the family shopping list. She told me I stank too, which didn't exactly help.

Mum knew her shopping list off by heart; it never changed, and had the exact prices for everything she bought in Tesco every Saturday. We kids went too, and she sent us running up the aisles to find each item as she ticked them off. It was 3 miles walk home, and we helped her carry the bags. Because she said I was "bigger boned" than Jocelyn I had to take the heavier bags, which pinched into my palms. I tried to swap them from hand to hand as I went along.

When we got home the military operation continued. Everything had its place in the cupboard, fridge or freezer and we would have to unpack the stuff onto the counter first and then into the correct spot. We knew we had to get it right, because if something wasn't where it was supposed to be my mum would start to shout at us. She policed the kitchen and it certainly wasn't the kind of cosy heart of the home you could wander into and make some tea or take a biscuit.

She would mark the contents of a cola bottle or a packet of custard creams with a pen so she could tell if anything had been taken by us. The amount of food purchased was calculated precisely so we would eat a set amount of everything week in, week out. We always had the same packed lunches, and she only ever cooked a handful of dishes for dinner, so she knew the quantities exactly. She didn't take the fact that we were growing up into consideration, so even as we got bigger and older we weren't fed more.

She could tell if a biscuit had been sneaked out by the way the wrappers were folded back, or if the packets in the cupboard were slightly out of alignment. This would spark a big row, and we'd all be lined up before my dad. No-one wanted to own up, as we knew we'd get punished. Father would interrogate us one by one until someone broke down and cried – usually because they were scared, and not because they had actually taken the food.

Dad would then haul them out and beat them, but that wasn't enough "discipline" for him because he also had to try to turn the rest of us against the "guilty party", playing us off against each other.

I managed almost never to cry in these line ups, by mentally removing myself from what was going on because I didn't want to give him the satisfaction of seeing me upset. I tried not to let him manipulate me and make me angry with the others, but I don't think they could always fight back that way and often they did just what he wanted and stonewalled the "offender".

At one point Mum started buying tins of broken biscuits and it got easier to steal fragments. Jocelyn,

Charmaine and I would smuggle them up to our room and hide them under the bunkbed to eat that night. We had lots of travel toothpaste which Mum had got from somewhere and as children we couldn't get enough of the taste of it. I would pinch a tube and use it to "ice" the bits of broken biscuit I'd squirreled away, smearing it on with a finger. I'd hide under the bottom bunk bed to eat them, with my hair getting caught in the springs.

All our evenings followed the same pattern. The moment Dad walked in the back door we'd get out of the kitchen as fast as we could to avoid getting the rap for his bad day (and it usually was a bad day). He'd stalk in, dump his toolbox on the floor, kick off his shoes and spit at my mother, "What's for dinner, how long and is there any post?" The same words every night for ten years. Forget "what's your day been like?" or "nice to see you."

Mum would fire back quick answers: "Meat and chips. Ten minutes and no." Then Dad would trundle into the living room on his rancid feet, take the remote from one of us and change the channel to watch the news. He didn't say anything to us, unless it was an order to make him a coffee. If we said anything about the news or whatever was on the telly he'd tell us to shut up, because "no-one cares what you think."

When the food was ready Dad would sit in state in the living room while we all ate in the kitchen. He only ate meat and gravy, and occasionally potatoes or chips, and he only drank black coffee with three sugars. He said he wouldn't eat vegetables because his own mother had forced him to eat them as a child, but boy, we weren't allowed to refuse to eat anything. "Wasting good food" was a crime as serious as stealing biscuit crumbs. It was a double standard he either didn't notice, or else loved upholding.

He'd come through to the kitchen and sit and wait for hours if necessary until we ate the last of the sprouts, or whatever they were. He'd also take the opportunity to bellow me out for holding my knife and fork in the wrong hands. I'm not left handed, but I've just always found it easier to eat with the cutlery reversed. He'd make me put them back in the "right" hands and then glare at me from across the table as I ended up with my knife in my mouth and tried to cut a tough piece of liver with my fork. This made me "an embarrassment" and "an attention seeker" according to him, and he'd round off by growling that I wasn't ambidextrous so had no fucking excuse.

Mum wasn't the greatest cook, and she either under- or overcooked most of the food, basics like chips and egg, ham and chips, liver and potatoes, or corned beef. It was enough to make me gag. Luckily we had dogs: Tina and her puppy Bear. They'd nestle quietly under the table, ready to take any food we couldn't eat and managed to slip under the table.

They were only fed once a day – half a can of food between them – so they were even more hungry than we were. They were cowed by my dad too, but they would still get under Mum's feet and then she'd kick them clean across the room. It made me cringe, and I'd try to coax them over to me so I could fuss them and stroke them until they'd stopped trembling.

We had a cat called Sox too, who was black with four white paws. I loved playing with him but one firework night my parents decided that he was too old and took him to the vets to be put down. I remember waking up the next morning and slipping downstairs for school and missing Sox who would normally emerge to greet me. I asked Mum who was standing at the sink in her dirty nightie where Sox was, so she told me flat. I started sobbing hysterically that I hadn't been able to say goodbye, and she told me to pull myself together and walk my sorry backside to school. And that was that.

CHAPTER 3

Scarred

I do have good memories too, because sometimes I was allowed to be a little girl growing up in the 1980s. My heroes were the stars of *Fame* and *Grease* and I watched the films on the telly over and over again whenever I had the chance. I longed to be older and to live the way the characters in the films did, and I'd dress up in my favourite pair of pink leg warmers, my pixie boots and a puffball skirt. I'd clip my hair up on top of my head and dance round the garden like the kids from *Fame* to Rick Astley and Bananarama.

If I could I'd spend hours watching shows like *The Wombles* and *Fraggle Rock*, and I loved the cartoons: *He-Man*, *She-Ra*, *My Little Pony* and *Dungeons and Dragons*. In the cartoons, "bad" characters always got their comeuppance, and good deeds and innocence were rewarded. I suppose they taught me the way things should be, even though in my home those rules were all turned upside down.

Our parents had pretty much cut themselves off from their own families – over the years Mum and Dad had been disowned by most of their blood relatives. There were no cosy Christmases with aunties, uncles, cousins and grandparents. It's difficult for me now to piece together who was whom. Mum did sometimes take us to visit her cousin's mum, and we called her "Little Nanny". She lived in a council house too, and had short, black, frizzy hair and glasses. She always seemed to be wearing a blue gingham apron when we went round.

Her kitchen had a wooden, fold-out table and she'd sit us all down and feed us beans on toast. I'd cover them in brown sauce and bolt them – I never liked the taste of baked beans, but I was always hungry enough to eat anything that was put in front of me. On the sideboard opposite the table was a miniature house made of matchsticks with perfect tiny details – windows, a door that opened and closed, a chimney – everything was in place. She'd built it herself and it had taken months.

We could never play with it in case we broke it, and I couldn't face upsetting Little Nanny, but I used to stare at it for hours and daydream about one day having my own house just like it. Then, suddenly, when I was still quite young, we just stopped going to see Little Nanny. I never knew why, but we didn't go back and I never saw the matchstick house again.

Like any child I loved to treat myself to sweets. When Sarina was old enough to have a part-time job she used to pay us 5p a week each from her wages for doing our chores. All five of us had to help Mother clean the house, though it goes without saying that Dad never lifted a finger. Our tasks were things like washing up, putting things away, wiping surfaces, walking and feeding the dogs, vacuuming the living room or mopping the kitchen floor and emptying the ash trays. On Saturdays and Sundays we had to finish our tasks before we could go out to play – if you remember that we were only let out of our bedroom at lunchtime, and given the fact that we had to wait for our parents to approve of the work we'd done, we wouldn't get out of the house till late afternoon.

When I did I would run straight round to the newsagent or the Spar and buy what seemed like an enormous bag of fruit salads, gobstoppers and sherbet space ships. Sometime they were rattled out of a big glass jar behind the counter into the weighing scale. Then I'd take them back home and hide them in my pillowcase to savour one a night until I could buy some more the next week.

At weekends Mum would yell at us to "get out from under my bloody feet and go play on the railway lines or in front of a bus! I don't care where – JUST GO!", so we really would go and play on the railway lines. We'd nip over the fence and through the garden of the old lady next door who couldn't chase us, and get on to the tracks. We'd play "Follow the Yellow Brick Road" on the sleepers, or search for slow worms in the debris by the track. Sometimes we played chicken, daring each other to run across the tracks when the train was coming. How we didn't get killed, I'll never know. No adult ever found out what we were up to.

We also played in the gravel pit, which probably wasn't much safer. There were huge heaps of sand and we could write our names in it and build sand castles. Most of the time we played out on the street with everyone else: Kirby, conkers and knock-down-ginger. We could mess around in the garden too, if Mum and Dad didn't mind the noise, but the overgrown grass concealed some nasty junk, as I found out the hard way when I was about ten.

Dad had an expensive hobby of keeping marine fish. These had to be purchased from a specialist shop and installed in a huge tank filled with salt water in a purpose-built cabinet in the corner of the kitchen. A fluorescent light flickered over the fish and a filter blasted bubbles to keep the water aerated. There were mini shoals of beautiful fish in all kinds of colours. I loved to watch them, they were so oblivious to everything that was going on in our house; I thought they had it easy! Mum of course never challenged him about the cost of the fish as he was kept entertained – or should that be distracted – and calm when he was looking after them and he left the rest of the family alone.

One morning we woke to hear Mum screaming to us all to get downstairs to help. It was a school morning, so our room had been unlocked and we hustled out of bed in a panic. In the kitchen there was a horrible scene – the tank had burst. A crack had appeared which had oozed water until the pressure was too great and it had given way, spilling the exotic fish all over the floor. Mum was frantically trying to pick up the flipping fish and putting them in saucepans full of tap water. We tried to help too but it was no use, and none of them survived the shock.

I steered clear of the house that evening until I could be sure I'd avoided Dad's initial, furious reaction. My parents decided that the jagged remains of the fish tank were too large to wrap up in newspaper and leave for the dustbin men to dispose of properly, so my parents' speedy (or lazy, depending on how you look at it) solution was to stick the remnants in the back garden.

A few months later I had a science assignment which involved collecting some flowers to press. We only had stinging nettles in our garden, and I didn't fancy nicking prize blooms from the gardens of anyone else on the estate, but I remembered that our neighbours had a large shrub which had purple flowers and grew right by our fence.

So I nipped round to the back of the house and picked my way through the garbage and long grass to a tree with branches that hung over the fence and the shrub. I climbed on to a branch and leaned along it so I could just about reach the blossom. There was a creak and a snap and the branch gave way. I flung out a hand to try and save myself and grabbed air and then another branch, which swung me heavily through a heap of rubbish before snapping and dropping me hard on my backside. I was still clutching the flowers like some kind of trophy but my school clothes were filthy and I started to brush at them frantically. Mum would kill me if they were dirty before the week was out.

When I bent over to lift up my skirt and check for cuts or bruises (blood would be impossible to shift) I felt a shooting pain up the back of one leg. There was a cut on the back of my right knee but the pain was coming from elsewhere. I twisted round to look and found myself gazing, in shock, at a six-inch long piece of glass sticking straight out of the right cheek of my bottom. The fish tank. It was covered in blood.

I pulled it out without thinking, and began to realise just how deeply it had jabbed in. I was in serious trouble. Dropping the shard and the flowers, I ran screaming into the house. Sarina was sitting in the living room watching a repeat of *Top of the Pops*; she frowned and tried to get me to calm down and tell her what was happening. When I turned to show her she leapt out of her chair and began yelling to Mum and Dad. By this stage the blood had soaked right through my skirt and was dribbling thickly down the back of my leg, over my white, rolled-down socks and into my shoes.

Dad had been out front working on the MG and Mum had been talking to him; she rushed in immediately. Mum turned white when she saw the blood; I was still screaming as I really thought I'd bleed to death there and then in the living room. Dad sauntered in and told us all to shut up, "What the hell is going on here?" When he saw the gore he quickly picked me up and rushed me into the kitchen in a fireman's lift. He ordered me to stand still and shouted at my mother, who was beside herself, to grab a tea towel and some masking tape from the junk drawer.

"She's going to need a lot of stitches in this", he muttered to her, taking in the laceration.

"Shall I ... erm ... call an ambulance?"

"Don't be silly, we'll stick her in the car and lay her flat across the seat", he said, sweepingly, trying to stem the flow of blood.

Mum tried to wrestle off my skirt and underwear as Dad held the tea towel in place. Then he began to wrap the tape hamfistedly around my waist to secure the thin cloth.

"This isn't going to work, Marge," he snarled, as though it had been her idea in the first place, "Get me another tea-towel."

The blood kept on oozing out, faster now, and soaked right through the "bandage". Mum handed him another cloth which he placed straight over the other which was now sopping wet and sticking to my skin. He wound on more tape as Mum stood there helplessly holding my skirt and knickers. I was dazed and getting lightheaded, trying to work out what was going on and why we hadn't gone to the hospital yet.

"Stitches, I think ... I don't want stitches."

"Yuck," Mum ignored me, "there's a whole lump of skin or flesh or something on her knickers."

She turned my knickers inside out to show the torn red flesh to everyone who was standing in the kitchen, gawping. I really lost it then, and started sobbing uncontrollably that I didn't want to go to hospital.

"I don't want stitches; just put a plaster on it!"

"Don't be so BLOODY stupid, Sam", my father snapped, grabbing my arm and hauling me out of the back door.

"Sarina, stay here and look after the kids; Marge, help me get her in the back of the car."

Mum scurried to obey and together they placed me stomach down on the back seat of the car, then climbed into the front. When we pulled up outside the hospital Dad carried me straight into casualty, pushed past everyone who was queuing at the desk and demanded that I was seen immediately. The nurse took one look at me and whisked us over to a curtained cubicle, telling Mum and Dad to hurry. Dad put me on the bed and then gave the nurse my details.

A doctor entered, pulled away the limp tea towels and set the nurse running around to fetch cotton wool and disinfectant. Mum explained what had happened and he nodded and said I'd need a tetanus shot. I had two injections into the open wound – one the tetanus and the other to numb it for stitching. Then they began to clean the cut and pick out more splinters of glass. Finally they stitched the sides of the deep cut together and the doctor told me not to bend over or to sit down until my stitches were removed in seven days.

I managed it but obviously after the stitches were removed I had an enormous scar and still do today. It took a long time to fade from purple to white and was sometimes even visible through my clothes. Nothing was done about the fish tank – my parents just left it out in the garden, and it was still there when we moved house, years later.

I got scared that once the stitches were gone I really would tear open the wound again, but it didn't happen. I suppose that was the kind of silly fear any child would get after such a disturbing experience but in our house our parents would never have responded by giving us a hug and explaining that everything would be alright. I was just told I was being an idiot, and they didn't try to reassure me.

CHAPTER 4

The war zone

As we couldn't turn to Mum and Dad for comfort we often behaved in a secretive and peculiar kind of way. When the Gulf War was looming the news had us transfixed. We thought that the jets and the bombs we saw on the telly would be heading for our estate. We didn't understand much of what was going on or that Iraq was so far away.

I got wound up because I knew we didn't have an air raid shelter and I didn't know where we would go when the attack started, so Charmaine and Jocelyn and I started to steal bin bags from the kitchen and to fill them up with everything we thought we'd need to survive – mainly our clothes and what toys we had. A child's idea of essentials!

We hid the bags in the bottom of our wardrobe because even though we were afraid that we were about to be bombed to smithereens, we were even more scared of Mum and Dad finding out. Every time we needed something we'd fish it out and then carefully replace it after use. It wasn't long before Mum spotted what we were up to.

"Why are all your clothes stuffed in those bags?" She demanded, suspiciously.

"In case we get bombed", I answered, straight-faced, on behalf of the others. They shifted behind me, nervously.

"Don't be so STUPID. That's in another country, not here, you wallies."

But it was all over the news and the paper. I didn't understand. She was having none of my excuses or worries.

"Unpack it all and do it before your father gets home and finds it and you all get a good hiding!" So we did, because suddenly getting bombed was less terrifying than the guarantee of being beaten by our father.

All very young children wet their beds, but if the problem persists there is often a psychological factor, and children growing up in a difficult environment are particularly prone to it. My father scared me so much as a child that I believe it's a major reason for the fact that I wet my bed from the age of seven until my early teens. I never told my parents because I'd seen how they treated Jocelyn who had the same problem.

She was diagnosed by the doctor with a "weak bladder" and prescribed pills and Mum would make sure she used the bucket before she could go to sleep. Father would just growl that she was lazy, and had no excuse. So if I woke up on damp sheets I'd simply pull a towel or coat under me, go back to sleep and then make the bed in the morning as though nothing had happened. No-one ever found out about it.

One morning when I was about nine I woke up suffocating under my bedsheets. They had been pulled right up over my head and tucked in so tightly that I could barely breathe. I was trapped under the purple sheets and it felt as though no air could reach me; the sunlight penetrated the cloth and my own trapped breath seemed to fill the space. I thought I'd die, and screamed to my sisters to help me, but they were too scared to move in case my parents heard the floorboards creak under their weight.

I struggled frantically against the sheets for what seemed like hours, but was probably only a few panicky minutes before the cloth ripped and I broke free, gasping for fresh air. I started to cry. The sheets had somehow got entangled in the springs of the bed frame, but how had that happened? And why were they pulled up so high, covering me entirely?

Dad bellowed through from his room, "What the HELL is going on in there?"

"Sam got stuck under the covers," bleated Jocelyn.

"I don't care. Shut up and go to sleep before I get in there and clout the lot of you."

Sniffing, I tugged at the bedclothes, trying to get them back in order. Charmaine was peering up at me from her bunk, looking worried; Jocelyn was glowering at me furiously, because she had been told off on account of my "fuss" and we'd all risked a hiding.

I never knew who'd remade the bed with me in it; I'd genuinely thought I was going to die, and was haunted by the idea that someone in my family had wanted me dead. I didn't sleep properly for weeks afterwards, scared that I'd wake up trapped again, or that someone would smother me with a pillow. Anything seemed possible in our house.

Once, after I'd apparently "answered back", Mother sent me to bed early. It was a Sunday afternoon and, being confined to my room I had nothing to do but sleep off the afternoon and stay there till morning. I woke with a start to hear her shouting upstairs: "SAAAAAAAMMMMMMMAAAANNNTHAAAA, hurry up and get down here." If I was "Samantha" rather than "Sam" it meant I'd done something wrong, so, running on fear and adrenaline I quickly threw my school clothes on and hurried down to the kitchen with my bag, thinking I must be late.

"What the hell are you doing?" demanded Mum.

It was still Sunday. Disorientated and trying to work things out, I stammered that I thought it was Monday

"Stupid fool," she hissed, "now sit your arse down at the table and eat your dinner."

Because we were told off for doing everything, and never praised for having done well, it was confusing to deal with grown ups who weren't our parents. At school I was wary of the teachers' reactions and kept taking precautions in case they got angry with me too. At junior school we had to report to the teacher's desk one at a time to have our work marked, so that they could go over the answers with us and explain the things we had done wrong.

Usually they started at the front of the class, so I realised that if I sat at the back they would run out of time before they reached me and would spend ten minutes going over the answers with the whole class instead. This meant that anything I'd got wrong was hidden, and the teacher didn't need to know. One day when I was about eight the teacher got wise to this and started to work through from the back of the class instead.

Maths wasn't my best subject and I didn't put much effort into my sums as I didn't want to ask for help and attract attention. When the teacher called me my knees went weak and my palms began to sweat and, heart pounding, I had to make my way to the front of the class to stand by his desk. I knew he was going to put a big red mark through my work, and I didn't know what he'd do to punish me.

Two sums down the page and there it was, I'd got something wrong. He began to explain the answer to me but I couldn't take in what he was saying; tears were welling up in my eyes as I nodded. Then suddenly, without any warning, I wet myself right then and there in front of the whole class and the teacher who was just sitting there staring at the puddle on the floor. I ran straight out of the room to the girls' toilets, where I tried to clean myself up, sobbing in humiliation.

Another teacher found me and took me to matron who gave me a clean pair of knickers and a skirt. Nothing was ever said to me by either my parents or my teacher, but every time I went to have my work marked after that, even when I was in secondary school, I remembered the horrible panic.

I did well in lessons on the whole, despite everything. My attendance record was superb because even if we were ill there was no-one home to look after us; Mum and Dad would both be out at work and there was no way they'd take time off. My parents called me the brainbox because I wasn't dyslexic, unlike all my sisters and Jacob. They didn't particularly care that the others had difficulty reading; when my mother told Dad that the others had been diagnosed as dyslexic he never even shifted from his seat in front of the telly. Eyes on the screen he delivered his verdict, "Dyslexia is just another excuse for being lazy." And that was that. Neither of them ever attended parents' evenings and none of the teachers ever seemed to care about that. Even with my good marks I wasn't happy at school when it should have been a haven away from home.

The other kids spotted that we were different and picked on every little thing. My packed lunch was one target. Every day I had the same thing, a sandwich filled with margarine and sugar, a piece of fruit, a packet of Tesco Value plain crisps and a snowball chocolate cake. They teased me because they said I should have had Walkers crisps, and Tesco Value was "tacky".

After a while I stopped eating in the canteen with everyone else and when the bell rang I'd rush off into the toilets and lock myself in a cubicle, sit on the lid of the loo and have my lunch alone. That was my solitary ritual. Occasionally the dinnerladies would come in to chase us out and they would peer over the locked door and spot me. Then I'd have to wait till we were back in our classrooms to have my crisps, smuggling them out of my bag and sucking them one by one when we were supposed to be reading. By secondary school I solved the problem by just eating my food on the way to school, but I'd be famished by lunch and would have to pinch everyone else's leftovers.

School uniform wasn't compulsory and we never had new clothes, so that was even more ammunition for the kids with designer stuff. Mum took us to jumble sales in residential homes and picked out what she thought was suitable from the mounds of old jumpers and t-shirts. She never gave us a say in it. When other girls pitched up at school in brand new jeans talking about what shopping centre they'd been to and what label trainers they had I'd just shrink away.

I couldn't lie about having amazing wardrobes full of beautiful outfits that I wasn't allowed to wear at school but I did lie about some things, partly so I'd just have something to say. I got quite cunning about spinning a story. Often I could just get away with saying very little and asking the other person lots of questions so they wouldn't notice I had nothing of my own to talk about. I needed my best, most elaborate tales when I got back to school in January and everyone was wearing their new gear and talking about all the presents they'd been given. I got very creative when I described our Christmases.

I'd say we'd hired a huge, beautiful hall which was decorated from top to bottom and full of balloons and toys. All our family came – aunties, uncles, cousins, grandparents – and we all sang, danced, pulled crackers and unwrapped piles of presents. Then we had a big feast and us kids would even be allowed a little wine. I thought that was the ultimate Christmas and would beat anything anyone else could come up with.

I was overcompensating big time, though, as nothing could have been further from the truth.

My father was a sworn atheist, so we didn't celebrate anything, not Christmas or Easter. He was, if anything, in an even worse mood at those times of year, and we had to creep around the house to avoid setting him off into a rage. Our friends on the estate were busy celebrating, so we couldn't play with them and we'd sit in the living room watching the same programmes when they were repeated every year, trying to avoid mentioning anything about Christmas.

I'd go up to our room and cry thinking about what other people's Christmases must be like. On the telly everyone seemed to be cheery and the image of a happy, loving family came up again and again. In the town centre I caught some of the buzz of the season looking at the lights in the street and the displays in the shops, but it only made home look more bleak.

Dad didn't like it if we disappeared upstairs and would grouse at us that we weren't "getting involved" and that we should sit in the living room, so it was back to the telly. If we tried to strike up a conversation he'd be furious, "Samantha, if I have to tell you one more time to shut up, then you will regret being born into this family." As if I didn't already! When I tried to read a newspaper he'd suddenly leap up, walk over and snatch it out of my hands with a "Shut up with that fucking racket! If you can't read it without making any noise you won't read the fucking thing at all!"

So we couldn't win, and pretty much anything we did would result in an ear bashing or even being beaten. On the other hand, Christmas did seem to be the one time of year when my Mum rallied and started at least trying to act like a normal mother. When I was ten she actually went so far as to put up some decorations in the living room. Dad's mood went from bad to apocalyptic. We could still hear them arguing about it when we were locked up in our room that night. Mum was crying and saying that it was for us children and couldn't do any harm. Dad said he didn't give a shit, and that we kids didn't deserve them and it was all a waste of fucking money. He thought she was just trying to copy the neighbours.

In the years after that, Mum sometimes dared to put the decorations up, and sometimes left them hidden, depending on his mood and hers. Some years she was defiant but often she didn't bother. I would feel really bad for her as I knew she was trying to make things right for us. I worried that I was ungrateful. We did at least get presents – that little bit of Christmas spirit did penetrate the household, but sometimes I wished they hadn't bothered.

Once my parents bought me a watch which turned out to be made of nickel, something they knew I was allergic to. This made me furious because of something that had happened a few Christmases earlier. That year, when I was about eight, Dad's father had given me a tiny set of silvery earrings in the shape of squirrels, which I loved as soon as I unwrapped them. When my Dad worked out they were made of nickel he dragged me round to see my grandfather and threw the little earrings back in the poor man's face, yelling and ranting at him that I was "fucking well allergic" to them. I was mortified and once more in tears, as I hadn't cared if I could wear the squirrels or not, I just wanted to keep them.

CHAPTER 5

Someone to turn to?

Perhaps the oddest thing about my childhood was the fact that our family's scary, isolated little world was allowed to carry on undisturbed. If our neighbours suspected anything or heard stuff through the wall, they didn't speak out, and Mum seldom had any friends round to see what the house looked like. They never made it upstairs and only came round when my Dad was out, too. Years and years later I had more contact with my parents' families and found out that they had suspected there were problems. My uncle once mentioned he had seen Dad kick one of us clean across the kitchen, and that they'd had a huge row about it, resulting in my uncle never visiting again.

My father's sister once told me she'd found us kids "strangely subdued" and meek, not like other children of our age were supposed to be. She didn't actually witness the abuse though, so had to keep her suspicions to herself. I only remember one time when it looked like we'd escape, and in fact we did, but it didn't last long.

I must have been about six or seven and still at primary school. I was sitting in my classroom halfway through a lesson when the head teacher suddenly walked in, had a word with the teacher and asked me to go with her to her office. My first thought was that I'd done something wrong, but she said nothing and took my hand and walked me out of the room and down the corridor with its smiley-face crayon drawings. I was anxious – what was going on? What had she been told? What had I done?

When we got to the reception area, I saw my mother sitting with Jocelyn, Charmaine and Jacob, who was only a toddler at the time. Mum took my hand from the teacher and dragged me with the others out the front door and through the school gates. She mumbled something about "going to stay with Nanny and Granddad", and that we could only take one thing each from home. I felt sure that we wouldn't be going back for some time, so begged to take two toys. She agreed hastily, but told us to hurry up, "Before your father gets home."

We chose our things quickly and followed her out to the bus stop where we caught one of the town's big cheerful yellow "Busy Bee" buses in silence. None of us asked any more questions. When we reached Nanny and Granddad's home they were ready to greet us with smiles and cuddles. We were settled in the living room in front of the telly while they took my mother, who had broken down in tears, into the kitchen.

Nothing was explained at the time, but my mother had finally cracked and run back home with us all.

She'd certainly never objected to anything Dad had done to us before. I found out the reason much much later. The night before when we had all been thrashed for our usual crime – talking in bed – Dad must have been especially brutal as the belt had left marks on Jocelyn which were still visible the next morning. One of the teachers at school had noticed the welts, and my mother had been summoned.

I don't know what she must have assured the staff at school if they didn't report the incident. I suppose she said she would take us and leave Dad and that we would be safe from him. It looked as though she was more worried about outsiders knowing about the abuse than the fact that it was actually happening. In any case, they let her go, and I don't remember any follow ups by Social Services. The teachers never asked me any questions about what went on at home, even after I returned to school a day or two later.

Mum didn't think to bring Sarina along with us too, perhaps because she was so much older, but perhaps also because she was only her stepdaughter. Her relationship with Sarina was strained, even worse than hers with me. So Sarina was left at home with my father. Years later she told me what had happened when they were alone together, and that awful knowledge was a terrible burden for me in my teens. It plunged the atmosphere of that house into something far darker and more sinister.

Of course I guessed nothing like that at the time. I just thought Father was probably angrier than usual, and the interlude at Nanny and Granddad's was one of the nicest periods of my childhood though we can only have stayed there for a week or so. It seemed much longer because it was so different to life in our own home. I was still scared that Dad might appear out of nowhere like a pantomime villain and haul us all back, kicking and screaming. I didn't want to go back to that terrible house, where we lived our lives in fear, never knowing when the next blow would fall. I didn't want to be hurt any more, and I didn't want to be back under my father's thumb.

At Nanny and Granddad's we sat down to eat together every night and were tucked up in bed with kisses and hugs. Mum seemed upset, but there were no arguments and my grandparents were happy to have us all under their roof. I really felt safe for the first time ever.

Granddad was round and jolly with a grey beard and a chequered cap which he never took off, indoors or out. He always had a pipe in his mouth which had to be stoked and re-lit all the time, and a big, fat, soppy brute of a dog who followed him round everywhere. Granddad already had my Nanny to look after full time as well as us, because she had been partially disabled by a stroke. Half her face was frozen and she had difficulty speaking, but I never found her scary, even though you might expect a young child would.

I never felt as close to my grandparents as I longed to be, though, because apart from that one week we didn't spend much time with them as I was growing up. When I was in my twenties I made the effort to get to know them better and to try and reconnect myself with that part of my family, but in a way it was too late.

One day during that week of escape my brother and sisters and I were in town with our mother; why, I don't know – we can't have been shopping. We were near the clock tower in the town centre when I suddenly saw Sarina running desperately towards us across the road, dodging cars as she scrambled to reach my mother. She flung herself at her and burst into hysterical sobs. I couldn't follow what was going on at all; I was pleased to see my half-sister again but that was cut short by seeing her in such a state. I don't know what they managed to communicate to each other then, but it was clear that something terrible had happened to Sarina. I knew it was strange that she should be clutching at my mother so urgently.

We must have gone back to Nanny and Granddad's after that and I suppose Sarina went back to Father. Nobody mentioned it that evening and I knew better than to ask any questions. I don't think that incident had anything to do with my mother's decision to take us all home a short time later – I don't know what the basis of *that* decision was. She knew exactly what he was capable of, and she had loving, forgiving parents who had welcomed her back into their house. But she still returned to him, and the whole incident – Jocelyn's bruises, our flight to Nanny and Granddad's — was brushed under the carpet forever.

I think she must live her life in denial; the only excuse I can think of for what she did was that she had become seriously insecure and that my dad knew exactly how to manipulate that. He could always get the upper hand by appealing to her somehow and I suppose she ended up feeling that she didn't deserve better treatment. He bullied her too, and sometimes she would turn to us kids and tell us she couldn't cope any more. When the next day came she would have changed her mind, and would start defending his behaviour to us — it was, after all, our own fault for making him angry.

I can appreciate that she had to work incredibly hard in dead-end jobs and that it must have been tough to deal with five kids on top of a tyrant like my father. But that's just the point. Who could stand by and let their kids be abused like that? And then tell them they deserved it? Ultimately she supported my father in everything he did and chose to stay with him while he made our lives miserable, and I cannot forgive her for that.

CHAPTER 6

Teenage rebellion

As I approached my teens I began to understand better and better how to deal with my family and to try and work out the easiest way to live in that house where anger and fear were common currency. But puberty also added a new and more disturbing dimension to our lives there, and a fresh threat just as I had begun to feel able to stand up for myself. My normal adolescent self-consciousness about my changing body was tainted with dread, and the strain of living with that took its toll.

As I went out into the world more and began to see just how different things could be, I grew more and more distressed at being trapped with my parents, because they seemed crueller and weirder the more I saw.

Simple things would upset me and throw me into doubt; I'd see other parents in the street holding their children's hands, the little boys and girls laughing and having fun. They weren't scared but relaxed and at one with their families. You could see the love that they had for each other and this was crushing to me as I knew I had never experienced that, and I was afraid I never would.

It's difficult for me, looking back now, to try and remember how it felt to be a teenager, alternating between lashing out and hating myself. I've worked through the events of my childhood in my mind and come to understand my behaviour better. I was scared and confused by how my parents treated me, and so young that I didn't know any other way of dealing with it. I had no real self-esteem to rely on. *It wasn't my fault.*

For most of my life, though, I believed that they were right and I was just a nasty, unpleasant person. It took a lot of work to realise that I wasn't so bad after all; it was just that my homelife had been so dysfunctional and unhappy and I had adapted myself to dealing with it. This left me completely out of step with the outside world.

Therapists believe that our parents condition us into accepting their own beliefs when we are impressionable children and when we enter adolescence we must begin to question things for ourselves and draw our own conclusions. If children aren't allowed to explore and experiment it becomes difficult for them to deal with many situations as adults.

My parents didn't give me any effective guidance; they didn't let me find things out for myself but drummed their own opinions into me over and over again. They never asked how things were going at school or chatted with me to help me work out for myself what I thought of something. It didn't matter if I had friends or not, and they didn't have any friends, so I didn't meet many other adults. Interaction in our house was confined to my mum and dad either telling us we were morons or ordering us to do something, and us either doing what we were told or answering back and getting clobbered for it. I didn't develop many social skills as a result. I couldn't be tactful, only argumentative and tough, because I wasn't expecting anyone to be nice to me. It felt like I had my fists permanently clenched.

Now I can be glad that I had that chippy, defensive attitude and I eventually hit back against my parents, but it took me a while to tone down that side of my personality when I needed to deal with other people! It allowed me eventually to cut my family out of my life before they could hurt me any more, and only then could I start sorting through in my mind just what an ordeal my early life had been.

It took me a long time to have any sense of perspective about my upbringing because for so long I lived from moment to moment, concentrating on how to survive in the immediate future rather than wondering how I truly felt or what I could do when I lifted myself out of that struggle. It's taken a long time to reach this point, and so many questions remain unanswered. They're the same questions I wrestled with as a teenager.

Why did my parents do what they did to us? Why didn't they hold our hands and comfort us, or tell us they loved us? Although I hated my parents for their behaviour, I couldn't fight a creeping sense that it was somehow my fault and that there must be something wrong with me too. I felt like I was a burden, an unwanted mistake. My parents weren't bringing us up, they were dragging us up, and they thought that was enough.

We had food, we had clothes and we had a roof over our heads. What else did we expect? They constantly drove home the point that we were "lucky" to have what we had and that others had less and would be grateful to be us. I knew that couldn't be true, who could want to live like this? But no, according to my parents we were ungrateful and we had more than they themselves had ever known as children, and we had no idea how hard life was in the big wide world outside our home.

I wondered why they felt they had to keep telling us that and sometimes I doubted my own instincts so much that I thought maybe we really were ungrateful after all. I still find it hard to fathom what they really believed. Perhaps they were trying to whitewash the guilt they felt about how poor the family was, and the way they had to keep scrimping and scraping for everything. Is it out of the question to think they might have felt guilty about how harshly they treated us in all those years of physical and psychological abuse?

As a teenager I was in a constant mental turmoil turning these questions over and over in my head, but there was no answer. There was no point in talking to anyone else about it, either. I managed to keep such a good "front" that even if I had really confided everything in friends or boyfriends they would have never believed what the reality of my family life was like.

All teenagers want to break out and rebel against their mum and dad, but to me as I plunged further into gloom it really seemed like a life or death fight, and the usual escape routes weren't open to me. There was no question of going to university or going travelling. I could imagine what my dad would have had to say about that! I didn't really plot about leaving home because I was worried about deserting the others, and I had, after all, grown up being told I was stupid and useless, so how would I ever survive on my own? Early on I considered running away several times. My dad just laughed at me: "You won't get very far! You'll be back again. What are you going to live on, anyway? Where are you going to sleep? You won't even be able to feed yourself."

No, it seemed to me that the only way to handle day-to-day life was to go to ground and bury my feelings. It was at this time that I really retreated behind my "mask" and began building myself an abrasive and, yes, "difficult" personality to cope. I had my own mind, my own emotions and thoughts, but even as a young teenager I was never allowed to express myself.

Anything I said was "nonsense", even if it concerned a trivial, inoffensive thing like a TV show and anyway I had a "serious attitude problem". After a childhood of being snapped at for so much as opening my mouth, I had learned that the safest course of action was to avoid thinking and talking about what was happening as much as possible.

If I didn't burst out and say something, I wouldn't be punished. It didn't make any difference what I did, anyway. All I had to do was to suppress how I really felt and push my emotions right down somewhere where I could only hope they'd stay buried. Maybe this was just giving in to the pressure my parents put me under to cage myself in and avoid being my true self. That was the last thing they wanted me to be. I felt like I was crammed into a small glass box, only able to peer out and silently watch what was going on in the outside world.

I didn't think I could get rid of my feelings any other way, and the idea of confiding in someone else seemed impossible. Besides, if I expressed my worries out loud, wouldn't that make them all the more real? If I didn't think or say I was sad, I couldn't *be* sad, could I? A combination of my treatment at home and bullying at school taught me that if I didn't get close to people, then I couldn't be hurt.

I blocked out any consideration of what might happen if the sadness came rushing back to the surface and swamped me. Given the fact that I was a volatile teenager and that tempers ran high in my house, sometimes my anger flared out and I found myself head to head with my dad. As you didn't have to actually do anything wrong to be punished in our family, my withdrawal tactics didn't always work. I also fell into jags of terrible, slow-burning depression which made the idea of having any kind of life at all seem hopeless.

There was a constant sense of not belonging – to my family, to any gangs at school, to anyone, in fact. If I let my attention slip away from the present, a terrible surge of emptiness would expand within me and make everything seem hollow and bleak, as if there was nothing behind the façade I'd constructed. Now, I know that that was the result of depression and I can handle it; then, I felt overwhelmed and lost.

There were some breakthroughs though, and my "mask" gave me enough confidence to try to turn my parents' fears against them. I was learning to manipulate them in return, and to "buy" some small freedoms for myself. I knew my parents were desperate for us not to answer questions that friends or teachers might ask about our homelife. Dad said we should keep our big mouths shut or we'd "be in for it big time."

Some people did have an inkling that all was not well and that we were being abused. One neighbour coaxed a few details out of me, and then went to my mother to ask her about it. Mum somehow fended her off, and I got a smack round the head for my troubles.

For a long time the threat held, because my dad backed it up by saying that if we did get "rescued" by Social Services everything would be much worse. We'd be separated among different foster families and then subjected to *serious* cruelty. Besides, I couldn't think of anyone who I trusted enough to tell and who was strong enough to stand up to Father and really take us away from that house forever. He loomed too large for that.

I thought that if Social Services came a-knocking at the door my parents would somehow blag their way out of trouble, spinning stories about how well cared for we kids were. And then, when they'd smiled and waved away the careworkers, they'd shut the front door and we'd be in *real* trouble.

So I couldn't tell anyone, but I could turn the threat against my parents and score a few victories. Mum was my first target; she was, after all, the softer of them, and the easier to exploit. I can't remember what exactly triggered my first rebellion, but I was sweeping the floor in the kitchen and had just reached the part where the ceiling sloped, by the under-the-stair cupboard. She was shoving me around as usual, telling me to do this and that or else she'd tell my father when he got home, standing over me with her hands on her hips, watching for dirt I missed. I was crying.

I just stopped what I was doing and turned to her with my face red and flustered. I felt a rush of confidence.

"If he lays one more finger on me I will grass him up to the police." I dropped my bombshell. Mother came right up to me and snatched the broom from my hands.

"Move it, out of the way", she snarled.

I moved hesitantly away from the cupboard, and stood beside her. I wanted a reaction to the bombshell, but I didn't want to end up trapped in that corner.

"I mean it, Mum. I'll grass him up to the police. And you as well, for that matter."

"Go on then, Samantha; they won't believe you anyway."

"Well, I'd rather take that risk, thank you very much. They will believe me if I show them the marks. Do your worst and see where it gets you both!" I was getting bolder by the second, exhilarated by a sudden surge of courage.

Mum pulled the dustpan and brush out of the cupboard, swept up the little pile of dirt and emptied it into the bin. She rattled the dustpan fiercely against the sides. Then she turned to see me still standing there, self-assurance rising, and said:

"Just get out of my sight."

That was enough for me. I trotted back to my room feeling grimly happy – she now knew I wasn't going to take it any more. And she'd have to work out what to do about that. It was a small concession but it was the beginning of a rebellion. My main target was the strict curfew that my parents enforced. We were supposed to be home by 7pm, no later, on pain of "indefinite grounding". This remained in place until we reached the ripe old age of sixteen, and I found it humiliating.

It meant I couldn't go on dates or to parties and I had to make stupid excuses to my friends which none of them understood. You could argue that my parents were trying to protect us, but that's too rich by half! We needed to be protected against them more than anyone else. At some point, my mum began to relent and let her favourite, Jocelyn, stay out till 9pm. I asked if

I could have the same right, and she gave me a flat "no". "She's older than you are."

"But I'm older than Charmaine and I don't get to stay out longer than her", I'd moan. Then I'd just stay out longer, and try to use the old excuses, that my watch was slow, or the bus was late, but my parents were wise to that and I'd get a good hiding and find myself grounded. Then Jocelyn started to date someone and my mother, astonishingly, started to cover up for her. When Jocelyn was out with her boyfriend, Mum would tell Father that she was babysitting for my aunt.

I was quick to grab the advantage this gave me. I asked her to cover for me too, and say I'd gone to my aunt's instead of my sister, and she refused. Then I turned her own best weapon back on her – I said I'd tell my father she was lying to him about Jocelyn. Then she knew she'd lost, and she reluctantly had to agree to let me go. This little bit of blackmail didn't impress Jocelyn, of course, as it meant she couldn't go out that night herself, and it put my mum in the difficult position of having to tell fibs to Dad, but I didn't care. I'd begun to realise that in our house, you had to look after yourself first, and snatch every opportunity that came your way. We were all pitted against each other and I couldn't afford to care.

My father was still the chief bogeyman, but after we moved house when I was fourteen we stopped getting beatings for talking after lights out, or for minor offences. I expect it was because we were getting too big, and even my parents had to acknowledge that the older we got, the less abuse we would take. Now I looked at him less with confusion than with out-and-out hostility.

He couldn't deal with situations in a civilised, honest manner, but always had to let rip at us. The flipside of that was an entirely false charm he could switch on sometimes for outsiders, which infuriated me. He would draw himself up and tidy up his speech – and cut out all the swear words he normally spewed out in every sentence. He'd give the impression of being amiable but stern, as though he wouldn't take any nonsense from anyone, and people bought this. I'd seen him purple with fury and thrashing the life out of one of his own children; so watching him strutting around and putting on these fake airs and graces made me boil, but of course it was best to keep my mouth shut. I suppose I thought that any decent person would see through him anyway.

I always hoped against hope that one day he'd pick the wrong person, and they wouldn't take kindly to his comments and give him some of his own medicine. That would show him, but for the time being he was still bigger than all of us and us kids seemed to be the only people who saw through him. He was a bully, and I think he really got something out of the physical abuse he inflicted.

His sadism came out in the way he needed to control everything about our lives too. Even though we were extremely well behaved on the whole because we were so scared, we could find ourselves getting punished for being good too. If we finished our chores and rushed off out to see friends, we'd get a nasty reception when we got home – a row and probably what they called "an indefinite grounding". The proper procedure must be adhered to: Mum or Dad had to inspect what we'd done and approve and then finally we could grab that window of free time before our curfew.

My father was capable of treating us well, but these episodes were rare and unpredictable. Once I bought him a fathers' day card and he really seemed pleased with it. I had only brought him one because no-one else had, and I hoped he would possibly come around to a normal, fatherly way of thinking. He patted me on the back and put the card on the mantelpiece and stayed in a good temper for the rest of the day. When he found out I was being bullied at school he "had words" with my teachers and also marched round to confront the fathers of the girls who were picking on me. These freak occurrences didn't endear him to me though – they were just baffling in light of his usual rages.

I hated mornings; waking up and thinking about the day ahead was painful. I'd drag myself out of my pit and face the world, always with the throbbing headache that plagued me for years when I was a teenager. The routine for the day was laid out before me in an unalterable pattern, each as dull as the last. My mum would be hovering downstairs, waiting for me.

When I dragged myself down to the kitchen there she'd be, bobbing around freakishly, feverishly looking for things to tell me to do. Pick up this, move that, do this, do that. My mind would be racing and I'd just want to be left alone so I'd keep quiet and turn on the kettle, just waiting for her to fire the first shot. My prayers might be answered if she still hasn't said anything by the time the kettle boils and the steam billows out. Can I get my coffee made and slink off before she can get a word out?

My luck would fail if she worked out a chore for me: "The tumble dryer needs emptying. Fold the clothes and take them back upstairs if that's where you're going." I'd know better than to argue and there'd be no chance she'd let me get breakfast and do things at my own pace. "Did you hear what I said?"

I'd give her a look. "Yes, *Mother*." Sarcasm was the closest I could get to telling her to get lost without guaranteeing a smack.

Satisfied, she'd bustle off into the living room, picking at my brother and sisters who'd be sitting around, eating their breakfast and watching the telly, "Empty the ash tray and wash up your bowls. Get a move on! You'll be late!" She couldn't help herself, as soon as she saw us she had to start nagging and moaning. She hadn't *got* anything nice to say and she couldn't make small talk. "Why can't you just do as you're told? Why do you always have to answer back? Don't be so fucking stupid!"

I'd pile up the dry clothes and bundle them into my arms carefully so I could still carry my cup of coffee, then head upstairs to get out of her range. The bickering never stopped. Once the clothes had been distributed to everyone's room, I'd wash quickly and dress for school, then make a dash for the back door before she can find something else to criticise. I'd grab my lunchbox as I flew through the kitchen and cram it into my bag. There'd be no "goodbye" or "have a nice day at school" – that would be risking more whinging from her.

Once the gate slammed behind me I could start to feel the tension that's built since the moment I opened my eyes begin to dissolve. My shoulders would come down from around my ears, my forehead would uncrease. I'd start to pick at my lunch, because I was still scared to eat the "cheapo" crisps and my sugar sandwiches in front of the other kids, who treated me like a freak. That was a whole new set of fears, but I found it easier to deal with those bullies than the ones at home.

The bullying I suffered as a child escalated in my teens, making school an even tougher place to be. I never really kept a "best friend" for long, and I'd lay the blame for that squarely at my parents' feet. I couldn't tell anyone about what was going on at home and that meant that they simply couldn't understand a large part of my life. It wasn't that I was too proud to reveal what I had to deal with, but I thought that I would only stand out more if everybody knew what was really going on, and then I'd just get picked on again. I wasn't used to sympathy.

Other kids would want to know why I couldn't go to sleepovers or parties when they invited me and, because I couldn't tell them the truth, they began to believe I didn't like them and moved away from me.

I was good at changing the direction of a conversation to avoid revealing things, but they would notice this evasiveness after a while. Some of my friends witnessed the treatment I got first hand, but never said anything about it to me. I think it embarrassed them. Either that or they were scared in turn and didn't know what to do.

Others used that opportunity to be spiteful. They'd say they didn't believe what I told them – which was just the tip of the iceberg – and I had no proof to back it up. They didn't hold back, calling me an attention seeker and a liar. When I did try and make small talk and avoid telling them what home was like, it was awkward because I had nothing "normal" to chat about, so I would borrow things that someone else told me to try and make my own life sound more interesting – this didn't help my reputation as someone who made things up.

They thought I just made up horrible stories because I wanted to be "special" and get noticed. The girls who took that line were usually the ones who had been my friends before turning on me, which only made me feel even more isolated. If people who were my friends did this to me, what was wrong with me? I wondered if maybe what was happening at home wasn't so bad and I was some kind of drama queen making a fuss about nothing.

I also had hassle from girls who didn't even pretend to like me. While some parents tried to keep their kids from being friends with our family, others let their children pick on us mercilessly. There was a huge crowd of girls who lived on or near my estate and who hung around together, talking. I'd be walking to school alone, and as soon as they saw me they'd fall silent.

Then they'd start to yell insults, "Chicken legs", "Smelly", "Cry baby", and tell me I'd "get a kicking" after school. They threw chewing gum at my hair. I'd have my hair pulled too, and be slapped and pushed about. Once or twice they even knocked me right over.

I couldn't concentrate at school because I couldn't stop wondering what they might be planning behind my back: a new nickname? Some other torture? I hadn't done anything to upset them, but I was vulnerable and they homed in on me. In PE they'd chant my name to made-up songs and say I smelt and had greasy hair and dandruff. There was one girl who'd try and sit behind me in lessons and cut chunks out of my hair. Not even the classroom was safe.

I tried not to rise to it, but when I did retaliate the teachers noticed and I'd get into trouble. The girls had a knack of twisting the story round so it was all my fault and they'd done nothing to provoke me. Once one of them came up to me and said she'd heard I was calling her names behind her back. I denied it and she called me a liar. My temper flared – if she was determined that I'd called her a name, why not just go ahead and call her something? So I called her a stupid bitch, and she told me to meet her after school to fight about it – which must have been what she wanted all along. She ended up being expelled because when we squared up later on she threw a punch which I never returned and, inevitably, my parents found out. My father stormed into the school, made his threats and that was that.

On the whole the teachers ignored what was going on, even if they were well aware of the intimidating behaviour of the gangs of girls. I assumed no teacher would care about helping me, so I never told them – I was more afraid of being labelled a "grass" and suffering the consequences. These, of course, were lessons I'd learned the hard way at home.

I just hated school, and willed the time to go by as quickly as possible, so I could get out and go to work instead. I didn't see it as a "wasted childhood". I tried to let the taunts and the attacks just wash over me, but it was no good – I just internalised it and ended up brooding over the harsh words for hours when I was alone. I let it get to me; I came to believe I really was the nasty person that everyone said I was, after all, no-one was saying anything to contradict that. I felt I had to deal with this alone.

CHAPTER 7

Being Supergirl

When the school day was over and I'd braved the walk home, all I had to look forward to was a miserable evening with my family nagging me and attacking each other. It seemed like I was sent packing to my room most nights, to "think about what I'd done wrong". I'd end up sitting on my windowsill trying to see what else was happening on the estate. Sometimes my mind wandered, and I'd drift off into my favourite daydream.

The film *Supergirl* had just come out, and I'd managed to watch it on tape from Blockbuster. I was engrossed. I loved the fact that she could fly, I loved her long, blonde, glamorous hair and I was entranced by her power – she was so strong! She seemed like the opposite of me as I saw myself – trapped, ugly and pathetic. I would perch on the sill looking down at the concrete a storey down below my swinging feet and wonder if, maybe, I could fly too.

I'd look up over the rooftops of the houses opposite and imagine myself soaring up there, heading away from the estate as fast as I could. I'd be able to see everything – everything below me and everything as far as the horizon and beyond. The wind would be swirling gently round me, my clothes flying out behind me. I would be free and nobody could touch me. When I took these "journeys" I really could forget about school and the other girls and my father and our miserable home. I was Supergirl and she didn't feel pain.

I'd be able to defend myself from my father's fists, from the buckle of his belt, from the cruel words. If he tried to attack me I'd catch his wrist and bring him up short, then with a quick push hurl him back into the wall, where he'd crumple into an immobile heap. Then he couldn't hurt me any more.

Coming back out of the fantasy was always cruel – I'd see the window as I "flew" back toward it looming larger and larger the closer I came. My bedroom was full of bad memories and as I sank back into reality all the pain I'd blocked out would come straight back. I'd try and tell myself it wouldn't be this way forever, and that if I could just stay strong for a bit longer I would get through it and be free.

Sometimes I picked dandelions from our back garden because I'd been told that if you blew all the seeds off in one go your wish would be granted. I'd pick handfuls at a time and blow wildly at them, begging to be anywhere but there, to be anyone else but me.

I had another dream that was all about being transformed and escaping, but I told my family about it and of course they just told me it was ridiculous. I wanted to be a supermodel and I could picture myself up on a catwalk with beautiful clothes and make up and skilfully coiffed hair, the flash bulbs popping. I imagined my face on magazine covers and bus stops, and photographers being in awe of my looks. I'd sign autographs for fans and have everything I wanted in life: a lovely house, a sports car, my own dogs, a partner, gorgeous children.

It was a pretty harmless fancy, but my parents always tried to squash it flat. "Don't be an idiot. You'll need a proper job. You're not tall enough and you don't have the right attitude, Samantha." In the end I kept the domestic side of my big ambitions – the caring partner, the house and the family – but dropped the part where I was a model. When I pictured myself up on the catwalk my parents' voices would sound in my head and it was impossible to imagine that I was beautiful any more.

When I was thirteen, my sisters and I were in town one day with my mum when a woman with a clipboard approached us. She said she was from a modelling agency called "Storm" and was doing a talent search. She was taking Polaroids of girls she thought had the right look to succeed. It was a lightning bolt for me, a real dream come true; I could hardly believe what was happening. But my mum wouldn't consider it, and just said "No."

She caught my arm and pulled me away from the lady, "We haven't got time for this. Move your arse." She marched off, dragging me with her, my sisters trailing behind. All afternoon I begged her, in tears, to let me go back and find the lady. I couldn't bear to lose the chance, and just didn't see what harm it would do to let me try. She was having none of it.

When my father got home that evening she told him I had played up in town and he decided to take me down a peg or two. He mortified me: he told me I wasn't pretty enough to be a model, I was much too young and I should concentrate on my school work instead. He rounded off by saying that while I was living under their roof I'd do as I was told and if I disobeyed one more time I'd get "the hiding of my life", then I had my backside slapped and was dispatched to bed early.

That was how things worked at home; we were constantly told that we must behave but there was no promise that if we did, we would be rewarded. We weren't allowed to aspire to better ourselves because that would mean we were "getting above ourselves" or "showing off". We were stupid if we thought we were going to make something of our lives. I think my parents thought that because their lives had been wretched, their own kids shouldn't have an ounce more privilege or ambition. There was no chance of them telling us to follow our dreams; it was like a life sentence.

I think what was left of my childhood innocence was killed when I was about ten, when Sarina confided in me about the things that had happened to her in the strange week when Mum had left Father and taken the rest of us to her parents' house. I barely understood or took in what she was telling me at the time as it seemed so awful, but the knowledge became harder to bear when I began to develop physically. There was no question of some kind of healthy, open attitude to puberty at home, and it was something that had to be dealt with furtively. I didn't want to attract attention to my new body at any cost.

My breasts, once they budded, grew faster than Jocelyn's despite the fact that she was older, and I remember my mother commenting that I was "clearly developing". That wasn't, of course, a cue for her to do anything about it and take me shopping for a bra, and I was too embarrassed to ask for one, so instead I hid myself in my old vests and crop tops.

A new bathroom suite had been installed in the house by the council, but that didn't mean we got to wash more often. Mum still saved money by making us share the same tub in turn. Before you could get in the bath you had to check that no-one else wanted to use the loo first; after that it was possible to have some peace and privacy. Except that Dad would always make a point of saying he didn't need to use the toilet, then, once I'd been in the bath for a few minutes, he'd start rapping on the door and demanding to be let in. I'd have to bundle myself in my towel and wait in the hall till he'd finished.

That wasn't the last of it. When he came out he'd try to rip my towel away for a laugh, so I'd be ready, clutching it with both hands, feeling sick to my stomach. I didn't find it funny, and I was sure it wasn't right. If I could I'd barge straight past him, slam the door and shoot the lock closed. I thought it was perverted, and worse when he tried to pass it off as a joke. When he was in a good mood he'd pretend he was hugging me, and reach for my breasts, then rub them up and down, laughing and "phwoaring".

Of course Mum knew about it; she was usually there to see it happen, and she'd just laugh along with him. Once I threatened that if he did it again I'd tell someone, but she told me not to be so pathetic. I didn't see so much as a flicker of fear or concern cross her face. His behaviour was made out to be totally normal and harmless, but it did have a lasting effect. I saw my body as something to be ashamed of.

A year or so after my breasts had begun to grow, I noticed a pain in the left one, which seemed tender and enlarged. I didn't know what it could be, but decided to try not to think about it – it must be growing pains. I kept quiet. I didn't want my parents examining me, that would be horrendous; obviously I preferred them not to touch me at all, let alone getting near my breasts.

The pain got worse though, and my breast started to look distorted, as if there was some kind of lump which was swelling. Jocelyn noticed and started teasing me – she said I had "deformed boobs" which were "pointy" and "cone-shaped". I got more and more self-conscious and really began to hate my breasts – I thought they were ghastly.

Sleeping became a problem. If I slept on my right side the weight of my left breast pulling down seemed to exacerbate the pain. If I slept on my left, it was squashed against the mattress. Lying on my front was out of the question. It ached steadily, with occasional sharp stabs.

After a few months the lump got even more obvious. I had to bathe myself delicately, carefully trying to avoid brushing against it as I washed myself. Dressing was hard too – lifting up my arm to put on a jumper made me wince. PE at school was difficult because I could barely run, having no bra of course made this worse still. I couldn't stretch to catch a ball. I had to take great trouble to keep out of people's way because a big blow would have left me doubled up on the ground. I thought someone was bound to notice.

I'd seen things on TV and in the papers about breast cancer and the idea that that was what the lump was began to take hold of me. Now I really couldn't sleep; what else could it be but cancer? I knew that there were machines to diagnose it, but what if it was too late? It's a measure of how terrified of my father I was that I decided I didn't care – I'd rather die than let my parents know about my fears. Then they'd both need to look, and I couldn't stand that thought.

It might be a blessing if the cancer just ate me away; that would be my escape route. Nobody could hurt me anymore if I died and I'd be free of my parents and my depression. So I said nothing and hugged my secret close to me. The lump thrived, and it was all but impossible to conceal it even under baggy sweaters. One day when I was walking out of the living room my mother walked past in the opposite direction and her arm grazed against my left breast and before I could help myself I screamed in pain. Everyone froze and turned to look at me.

My mum demanded to know what the problem was; I told her, lamely, feeling defeated. Her face turned white. She insisted that I show her my breast straightaway and I hesitated, knowing this would mean a trip to the doctor or the hospital, and being stripped naked and prodded by strangers with my parents gawping on. When she saw me stalling Mum yelled to my dad hysterically that I had a lump in my breast and wouldn't let her look.

The numbness turned to dread; I didn't want this. I hadn't asked anyone to look, this was my secret, why wouldn't they just leave me alone? My dad approached and snarled at me to remove my sweater and show him the growth immediately. Mum stood behind him, chewing her finger nervously.

There was no point arguing. I pulled my jumper slowly off. I refused to do some kind of striptease for him though; I kept my crop top on, but pulled it a little to one side to reveal the swelling. There it was, in all its horrible glory, my "pointy", "cone-shaped" breast, capped by the gross, distorting bulge.

Mum started to panic, "How long has that been there? Why didn't you say anything?"

Dad just said, "I need to touch it, Samantha; I need to see what it feels like."

I turned away and tried to focus on the wall on the other side of the room. I knew I'd have to suffer this final, creepy humiliation now. The game was up. I felt his cold, rough hands touching and squeezing my breast. He pinched me, feeling around the lump. I felt a wave of nausea building inside me. Then he said he had to see my other breast, "in order to compare them".

As I miserably pulled down the other side of my top my mother was on the phone, frantically dialling the doctor's surgery and shrieking that we needed an emergency appointment because I had a tumour on my breast. She put the receiver down and said we had a slot straightaway, and I pulled my jumper back on, feeling wretched. Mum and Dad hustled me into the car to drive to the surgery and, while he waited in the car park, Mum rushed me officiously into the GP's room, with a look of frantic concern pinned to her face.

Again I peeled off my top and let the doctor look. For a few minutes she said nothing as she gently pressed and prodded it. I flinched with every touch. Then she told me kindly that I could get dressed again. She turned to my mother and said confidently, "It's nothing to worry about, just a milk gland that's got blocked." My mum sighed ostentatiously and her shoulders relaxed. I was prescribed some tablets and the doctor reassured us that this was quite a common problem in teenage girls and that I should get properly fitted with a bra because it would help a lot.

As we walked back to the car Mum paced off in front of me, knowing my dad would be boiling over with impatience, and that he wouldn't be impressed with this good news. I was in a daze, embarrassed at having caused such a fuss and mortified by the fact that my father had been groping my breasts. I barely heard anything they said on the drive home – they were talking as though I wasn't even there. I stared out the window, outraged that it hadn't been cancer, and that I wouldn't die after all.

CHAPTER 8

My punishment

One Saturday I went into town for a few hours with some girls I knew. I had no money to spend, but I didn't care as I'd do anything to get out of the house. After lots of window shopping and trailing from place to place we all congregated near a stairwell with another bunch of teenagers. At the top of the stairs was the entrance to a restaurant and some of the kids were yelling comments up at the customers, like "You know when you've been Tangoed!"

Suddenly they legged it, leaving me and my friends doubled up with laughter. A hand slapped down heavily on my shoulder and yanked me round so fast I nearly lost my balance; I was face to face with a woman who was glaring at me ferociously. She had a frizzy auburn perm and when she spoke I was almost knocked over again by the stench of garlic on her breath. The other girls took one look and ran, leaving me there with the woman's nails sunk right into the skin on my neck.

"What the hell are you playing at?" She started to shake me violently.

"I wasn't doing anything!"

"Don't lie to me, you little cow! You were screaming *shit* up the stairs, annoying all my customers." Her spittle hit me in the face.

"Let go of me!" I clawed at her hands desperately

"If you dare come back here and annoy my customers again, you little bitch, I'll make sure you pay for it."

"You've got the wrong person", I pleaded, but she didn't care, there were no other kids around so I was taking the blame. By now lots of people had gathered round to watch, but no-one stepped in and did anything. The woman dropped me and stalked back up the stairs, and the crowd of onlookers all lost interest and carried on with their own business as if nothing had happened. Mum and Dad had always taught us that we should call the police if anyone else tried to hurt us, so I did just that. I ran to a phone box and dialled 999.

"Police, Fire or Ambulance?"

"Police, please." I muttered, still quivering with shock. My neck was scratched raw and had turned a burning red.

"Hello, you're through to the police, how can we help?" said a stern male voice.

"A woman's just attacked me," I stammered, then described what had happened for him. He told me to wait where I was and that a policeman would be along in a few minutes. While I waited I thought I should phone home to tell my mum what had happened. My father answered and accepted the reverse charged call from the operator so I had no choice and had to tell him. He didn't say much; he just growled that I had to get straight home as soon as the police finished with me. I knew I was in deep trouble.

The policeman found me and asked what had happened. I tried to tell him, but I had no witnesses to back me up. He took notes for five or ten minutes and looked at the marks left on my neck. Then he told me to take him to the woman who had done it. We went back to the stairs and made our way up. I could see the woman in the restaurant through the glass doors at the top and pointed her out. I held on to the policeman's arm, scared about what was going to happen.

She spotted us and stepped outside, looking worried but with her arms folded firmly. She and the policeman walked off together to discuss what had happened. When they came back, the policeman told me he wasn't going to investigate any further, and that I should get home. The woman looked smug. She went back into the restaurant and I sloped back to the house trying not to think about what was waiting for me.

Mum was at the sink. She looked back over her shoulder at me and just said, "Your father wants a word with you, young lady." I raced upstairs as fast and as quietly as I could and hid in my room, holding my breath.

"SAAAAAAMAAAANNNNTTTTHHHH-HAAAAA! Get your backside down here this moment." My mum bellowed up the stairs. There was no escape. I inched down, step by step, my hand clammy on the banister. I walked into the kitchen and looked at her solemnly, "Yeah?"

"Didn't I say your father wanted a word with you?"

"Yes," I replied meekly.

Dad came storming in, his face set. I moved swiftly out of his way and propped myself against the wall, feeling powerless and cornered. Mum was stirring some potatoes on the stove; Jocelyn had been sitting at the table talking to her and she was now frozen to the spot, too scared to leave. Dad turned to me.

"Why didn't you come into the living room when you were told to do so by your mother?" he pointed his finger aggressively at my face, eyes blazing.

"I don't know", I said softly, my insides turning to mush. I looked down at my feet.

"So you go into town, start trouble, call the police – who by the way have been on the phone to me telling me that this woman denied everything – then come home and run away to bed. You hide from me without talking it over and you expect me to be pleased with you?"

"But I didn't do it. It was someone else." This just made him angrier, he couldn't stand a liar and he didn't believe a word I said.

He grabbed my throat and began to squeeze, shoving me back and pinning me against the wall. He was much bigger than me and his hands felt like they went right round my neck. He then lifted me off the floor with one hand, pushing me up the wall by my throat until I was face to face with him. I was struggling to breathe, my lungs sore; my face was squashed up by the pressure of his fingers and I could barely open my mouth.

My mother carried on cooking calmly. Jocelyn was petrified; I tried to signal to her to help me with my eyes but I knew it was hopeless as she couldn't afford to get involved. I could see tears starting to run down her face.

"This is the last time I'm telling you about your attitude, Samantha." My father ground out through his teeth, pressing harder still. My feet dangled inches from the floor.

"I … can't … breathe!" I could feel myself getting light-headed and grabbed at his hand to try to pull it away. It was the first time I'd tried to fight back against him as I knew that the others couldn't or wouldn't do anything to save me.

"Pack it in!" He shook me and strengthened his grip again. He stank of stale cigarettes and black coffee, and his pupils were dilated and black. His face had turned red with effort and fury and a vein had started to bulge on his forehead. He could see the fear in my face but it had no effect on him; I was helpless. I could hear Jocelyn whimpering in fear but I couldn't make out what Dad was saying to me for lack of oxygen.

Mum turned round and wandered over to the sink for a tea towel. I thought she might say something or stop him, but she just wiped her hands on the towel and stood there to watch.

"Tell me what you think!" He roared, his nose so close to mine that it was almost touching, "Tell me what you think of me!"

I could only think of breathing and I knew I was going to black out any second, but something came welling up in me as I struggled, something that was outrageous and totally true, but I couldn't stop myself now.

"I FUCKING HATE YOU!"

His jaw gaped and his eyes stared in sheer disbelief as he stood stock still for a moment, his hand still pinioning me above the kitchen floor.

"I told you to tell me what you thought of me, not to swear!"

By now I was beyond caring, I had had enough and I thought he really was going to kill me so I'd rather die fighting. I didn't care about the repercussions anymore and I was glad I'd had the satisfaction of finally saying that to his face. I'd had enough of creeping around and biting back everything I really thought. I had let him have it, for once.

Then he loosened his grip and just turned and walked out of the kitchen. I slithered to the floor and clutched at my throat, inhaling deeply to suck air into my lungs. Everything was spinning and I couldn't understand what had just happened. Mother looked down at me.

"You had better get up to your bedroom and stay well out of his way." I stared at her, shaking my head, and got slowly up and did just that.

I had thought a mother's love, even *my* mother's love for her children was an unbreakable bond and that a mother would do anything to protect her children, but she had once again left me to suffer the worst that my father could dish out. Perhaps he attacked her too, but I was never aware of it. If my own child had been abused before my very eyes I know that I would have done something to protect them, but I had now run out of excuses for my mother. She would never be there to support me or save me. I didn't see much use for her after that; as far as I was concerned I was on my own.

It was really strange, but sometimes she would actually turn to me for support. If Dad had been especially mean she would start telling me, "I cannot live like this any more", and expect me to act the adult and comfort her. I'd suggest that she left my dad once and for all and that we would all go with her and it would be ok, but she always dug up some excuse, and I got tired of offering the same, rejected advice. I knew my grandparents would have taken her in. That had happened before. I gave up and let her cry on my shoulder till she wiped her eyes and dried her glasses on the nearest tea towel. Then she'd tell me to "go and play in the garden" as if I were five years old.

Her threats of punishment meant less and less to me as I grew up, partly because I could blackmail her about the lies she told Dad and partly because I think she feared the anger he would act out on us for the smallest misdemeanour. Perhaps she thought it would be turned on her in time. She lost her temper too, though, and would chase me with a slipper, whacking my legs. She never held back then.

I'd lock myself in the bathroom when she got carried away and thrashed me too hard, and after a few hours she'd start apologising profusely and telling me it was my own fault for pushing her too far. I think the apologies were more to reassure herself than me. She'd never take responsibility for her own violent behaviour if she could help it.

One day I stopped running away. She'd slapped me hard in the face for "answering back" and I swung back in return, catching her smack on the cheek and leaving her greasy hair pasted to her skin. She just stood there in shock, gazing at me, then turned without uttering a word and walked back to the hob where our miserable dinner was cooking. I was torn between guilt at lashing out and defiance, but in the end I felt that I owed her nothing. I'd tried sympathising but she wasn't prepared to leave Dad and protect us all. At least this way I could protect myself. Anything more than that seemed impossible.

CHAPTER 9

Finding a way out

In the end I found another way to escape from the terrible atmosphere at home. I was fourteen when I met my first boyfriend, and I thought I'd found the solution to all my problems. My friend Diana had invited me to a party, which sounds unremarkable for a teenager but was incredibly exciting for me. My father didn't let us go to parties where there would be boys and alcohol – he would rip up and bin any invites we tried to show him for approval.

I planned my moves carefully. I left a bag of clean underwear and my favourite clothes at Diana's house on the Friday night when I walked back from school. Then I asked if I could have permission to stay at Diana's on Saturday – just the two of us, having a girly night in. My father graciously agreed that I was allowed out for the night, but he searched my bag before I went, as I knew he would. He launched into a huge lecture about behaving myself which wound up with the usual covert threat about what would happen if I didn't do exactly that, and then I was out of the door, bag over my shoulder.

At Diana's we spent hours glamming ourselves up. I'd never tried a full face of make up before and she showed me how to put on foundation, eyeshadow and liner, blusher and mascara. I squeezed into a tight pair of black trousers and a tiny top that skimmed my belly and, encouraged by Diana, helped myself to her perfume and deodorant too.

I was beginning to feel like the proper teenager that I'd daydreamed of becoming – the kind I'd loved watching in *Fame* and *Grease* when I was little. This was a new kind of exhilaration, an excitement that something good was going to happen. It was still tinged with apprehension – there was no way I could get drunk or my dad would definitely guess and I'd never be allowed out again. He might find out where I'd really been, and then I'd be beaten badly. He'd cause a scene with the parents of the kids who were holding the party and then I'd never live it down at school.

When we got to the house it was already heaving with people, and there were lights all over the garden. Toilet paper was strewn over the trees and music came thumping through the walls and rattled the windows. Kids were sitting on the front doorstep clutching beer cans, taking a swig then wiping their mouths with the backs of their hands. Girls in tiny skirts were flirting with boys, holding a cigarette in one hand and a wine glass edged in lipstick in the other. Diana and I pressed our way through the throng and made for the kitchen, where there were rows of bottles of every kind of booze imaginable.

A boy with a big cheesy grin sauntered over, he introduced himself as James. He gave us each a glass with a dodgy-looking potion in it – I don't know which of those drinks on the kitchen side it had been concocted from, but we drained our cocktails quickly, desperate to catch up with everyone else. I hated the taste and was scared about getting drunk. My parents liked to tell us girls that if that sort of thing happened at a party we'd probably end up getting raped – that was the kind of big bad world stuff they were trying to protect us from by stopping us going out.

Being out like this was scary enough, so I didn't drink much more. I was paranoid that Dad would smell the stuff on my breath the next day too, and then he'd go ballistic. I spent the party in a state of equal parts fear and elation, feeling brave but terrified too.

The party seemed to be going on in every room in the house, and Diana and I danced our way round them all, puffing away on our cigarettes and daring each other to chat to boys. Diana was better than me, maybe because she'd drunk more, but I suddenly caught sight of a guy sitting on the staircase, swaying a little and staring down into his beer can. I thought he was gorgeous.

He had big brown eyes and short dark hair which was cropped so it fell forwards. He was very smartly dressed too, in a white shirt and blue jeans. I pinched Diana's arm and pointed at the boy.

"He's lovely", I whispered.

"Go 'n' talk to him, then", Diana slurred back, dangling off a boy she'd started dancing with about five minutes beforehand. I suddenly felt very, very young; I couldn't think of anything to say to the boy, but I knew I had to find the nerve somewhere. What if I didn't get to go to another party again, or what if I never saw him after that night? I walked gingerly over and plonked myself down next to him.

"Hi", I said confidently, in his general direction.

"Alright", he replied, glancing up from his beer to see who was speaking to him.

"Good party, isn't it?"

"S'alright", he said, chewing gum furiously, "but I think I've had too much to drink now."

"What's your name?"

"Peter", he said, "What's yours?"

"Sam", I smiled. "Nice to meet you, Peter."

The party was starting to wrap up now, and I thought I might miss my chance to make an impression, fast. I pulled the can of beer from his hand and leaned in to press my lips on his. He pulled away, surprised. My stomach dropped, I'd really blown it now, how stupid could I have been? But then he just picked the ball of chewing gum out of his mouth, dropped it in the beer can and began kissing me back, passionately. It was my first kiss, and I was bowled over. I came back down to earth pretty quickly though, as Diana was tugging on my arm. We had to go.

Peter and I hastily agreed to meet up the next day at lunchtime at a laundrette a few minutes walk from

Diana's house, far enough from my house to be safe. That night on the camp bed at Diana's I couldn't sleep. The thrill of meeting Peter and kissing him was replaced with doubt and plain, cold complications. Dad wouldn't want me to have a boyfriend. I still had my curfew, how could I explain that to Peter? I had no money. I was only fourteen and still shuttling between school and my parent's home. What would Peter see in me? I thought he couldn't possibly be interested in me; my bravado evaporated.

The next day I was at the laundrette, though, fuzzy with lack of sleep and desperate to see Peter again, whatever happened. He pulled up bang on time on his motorbike, a buzzy little 50cc, pulled off his helmet and smiled and everything was suddenly ok. I knew it was all going to work out just fine, and I broke into a big grin. After that we were boyfriend and girlfriend, something I'd hardly dared hope for only a few days ago.

He was seventeen and I was only fourteen, but felt older than my years. I was still socially inept, either withdrawing into myself or being excitable and overconfident, but Peter took that all in his stride, and when I was with him I began to blossom. I took the precaution of introducing him to my parents, as word on the estate would have reached them sooner or later, and if they'd thought I'd been sneaking around behind their backs it would have been far worse for me. He met my mum first as I knew she'd be easier to handle. Then I briefed him on what to expect from my father.

He wasn't to "answer back" to him or disagree with anything he said; he mustn't challenge Dad's curfew for me and he had to understand that he couldn't let on that we had met at a party or that I'd been drinking at the time.

Father put on his usual stern act, sizing up Peter and asking him, "What are your intentions with my daughter?" Peter refused to rise to the bait, and played his part well; Dad couldn't rattle him, but he couldn't fault him either, and gave us his blessing, grudgingly enough. There was no change to my 7pm curfew, but I could still snatch the odd night out by getting my mum to pretend I had been babysitting for her sister again and for the time being this was enough for me.

I was head over heels in love with Peter; the uncomplicated passion of a first love was amplified for me because I had felt so alone and low before I met him. There was no other person who loved me, so I clung desperately to him; it was the most intense feeling I'd known. When he wasn't there I missed him feverishly. I wished away the hours, and raced out of school, gulped down dinner, hurried through my chores, counting down the seconds till I could be with him again.

I didn't want to tell him everything about home in case he decided he didn't want to take on the burden of all my problems, but there was no chance of him not guessing some of it. He'd see the bruises. I turned to him for advice on how to deal with my dad. I needed excuses to stay out later, and permission to ride pillion on the

50cc, something Dad had out and out forbidden me to do.

The feeling that there was someone in my life worth caring for and who cared about what happened to me and what I felt and thought was brilliant, and I was addicted to it in no time. I wrote him reams of letters when I was stuck back in the house after the curfew had passed. I craved his attention 24/7 like a drug, and he seemed to appreciate my need rather than being disturbed by it. He never complained.

At last I had someone to talk to about – well, anything, things that didn't matter so much, like motorbikes, school, worries about exams.

After we'd been together for about six months I lost my virginity to Peter; he was very gentle and caring and I never regretted it. I was under the age of consent, but as far as I was concerned it was my body, and as long as I didn't get pregnant nobody else needed to know.

Then there was a disaster – my period was late, first by a few days, then a week, then two. I panicked and booked myself an appointment at a walk-in centre for a test. I didn't tell anyone about it. My dad had told me a few weeks beforehand that if I got pregnant he would "kick the baby out of me". I was fourteen, how would I be able to cope with a baby, in a bedsitter somewhere? What was I going to do, run away? Throw myself down the stairs? Take a hot bath with gin? I had wild thoughts about concealing the bump under baggy clothes as I had done with my breast lump but surely morning sickness would be a giveaway? And what would happen when I went into labour? I felt sick all the time, but I didn't know whether it was with worry or because I was pregnant.

On the morning I was due to go to the clinic, my period started and I almost collapsed in relief. I was determined I shouldn't go through the same thing again, though, and went to see the family planning doctor anyway. She suggested that I go on the Pill and reassured me that my parents didn't need to know about it. So after being weighed and having my blood pressure taken, I got my boxes of pills and took them home to hide under my mattress. I was learning to look after myself, and finally being able to take at least one part of my life into my own control.

Free of that fear, I could relish being smitten with Peter, and we managed a year of juggling my curfews and dodging my parents. His parents were very accepting of me, and would invite me round for huge Sunday roasts and ask questions about how I was doing at school and what I thought about this and that. It was all very different to home, and I really felt like I had the beginnings of a life away from my family.

CHAPTER 10

Overwhelming pain

Nearly a year after I met Peter I underwent a traumatic operation which left me miserable and wheelchair bound. It also hardened my feelings against my mother, because I ended up holding her personally responsible. I'd always had problems with my toenails and they had a tendency to grow right round and into my skin. It was incredibly painful and one summer it escalated into a major problem when my big toenails became infected and yellow puss started oozing out from under them.

My doctor referred me to the hospital to have them sorted out and my mother took me to my appointment. We were sitting waiting in a corridor when the sounds of a man, a grown man, screaming in agony rang out from the consulting room. It carried on for about twenty minutes. My mum didn't comment. I sat next to her and felt panic rising through me, and tried not to imagine what was happening in there.

The door opened, and a man in his twenties came hobbling out on crutches, tears in his eyes. One foot had a huge bandage on it so I guessed that he must have had his big toenail removed. I didn't like to think how

I would cope with what was coming next because I knew the doctors were probably going to remove both my big toenails. If he couldn't hack it, how would I?

I started to tell my mum I wouldn't go through with it, and jumped up as best I could on my infected feet to leave, but the nurse at the door of the consulting room called my name and Mum took a firm hold of me and tugged me towards her. I went to pieces, shaking and screaming. I hit out at Mum, and the nurses and doctor moved in to try and calm me down, but it was no good. I didn't trust them for one second! I'd heard with my own ears what would happen to me; I didn't want them touching my feet.

They picked me up and lifted me on to the operating table. One nurse took hold of my left arm, another the right. There were two nurses holding each of my legs and my mum just sprawled across my middle, pressing down on me as I struggled and yelled. The consultant readied the local anaesthetic to numb my toes.

"Can you feel this?" He prodded the tip of my toe with something that felt like a scalpel.

"Yes! I bloody well can!" I screamed in tears.

"Nurse, more anaesthetic, please." My toes tingled at the prick of the second needle.

"Just think," said the nurse holding my right arm, "This time next year you'll have lovely toenails and you'll be walking along the beach all proud of them."

The doctor clamped my feet against his stomach and began tearing away at my toenails. "They will both have to be removed entirely." It was murder, the anaesthetic didn't seem to be working at all, and I kept up my screams.

"She can't feel a thing," the consultant told my mother, as he clamped something onto the nail and started tearing away at it, "That's all the local we're legally allowed to use."

Hate welled up and flooded my system. Why wasn't my mother doing anything to help me? I was in agony and she just took the doctor's word and was actually helping to pin me down. My pain meant nothing to her. She was totally unmoved and only spoke to tell me off for fighting.

When they were finished I was bandaged up and installed in a wheelchair. Mum rushed me, still weeping and in pain, down the corridors till we got to the car park, then she slapped me hard around the head and snapped, "What do you mean by making all that racket and embarrassing me in front of all those people?" We drove home without a word. Mum told Dad that I'd made a big scene for no good reason.

It was the summer holidays and my orders were to keep my feet raised at all times so I had to stay indoors while my sisters were out playing with our friends. My toes alternately throbbed and stung and the bandages were so big they pushed my other toes sideways. When I looked at them they reminded me of a cartoon – Popeye, after he's whacked his thumb with a hammer. I couldn't wear shoes for two months and even then a big pair of soft trainers left me sore.

After a month or so I was allowed to progress to crutches some of the time and they were hard work. I had to go slowly or I'd lose my balance, but at least I was excused my chores. The district nurse came round every second day to change the dressing and clean my toes. I'd sit on the sofa and soak my feet in a bowl of warm, salty water as she gently eased the remains of the wrapping from the tender skin where my nails should have been.

One day she was away so a replacement came, who had a different method – she just ripped the dressing right off, making me scream out loud. At this point my mum came racing in and started shouting at the nurse, and nearly threw her out of the house. After she'd coldly watched me suffer in the operating theatre, she had apparently decided to care. Perhaps it was show for the nurse. I certainly didn't take it seriously; I was still smouldering with hatred for what she had done in the hospital.

I felt even more justified a few months later when my toenails started growing back and I was sent to see a chiropodist. This specialist took a long hard look at my feet and then checked my records. "You didn't need to have your toenails removed," she said, finally, "they should have just cut a 'v' into them to stop them growing into your skin. It would have taken longer, but it would have hurt less."

So what had happened? Had Mum just taken the easiest option, thinking that an operation to wrench my toenails off would be quicker than the gradual treatment? I thought when I heard that that she probably hated me so much that she enjoyed seeing me in pain. After all, she had never lifted a finger when Jocelyn, Charmaine and I had been beaten. It was an odd thought for a fourteen-year-old, but was perfectly logical to me. Of course it was deliberate, I reasoned – my mother hated me. The fact that she'd bawled out the district nurse was much stranger as far as I was concerned.

When I told my mum what the chiropodist had said she just said it didn't matter any more and we couldn't turn the clock back. After that I pretty much gave up thinking of her as a mother. My nails grew back thick and rippled, with a nasty yellow colour and I still have problems with them so that horrible afternoon in the hospital and the months of recuperation all seem pointless now.

My sister Sarina also had problems with her feet, and still does. The longest toe on each foot curled right under the balls of her feet and eventually made walking difficult. She had a deeply painful operation too, and the surgeons inserted metal rods into each toe to straighten them. Back home she was in agony, but I don't remember Mum or Dad showing her any compassion.

Sarina told me that she thought the problem was caused by having to cram her growing feet into the shoes too small for her. My mother refused to buy new shoes until the soles were completely worn out, so Sarina's feet were as crushed as if they'd been bound like a Chinese girl's. Her operation wasn't very successful either, so she too suffered appallingly for no gain at all.

I don't remember Sarina being treated with much respect in my family. I've already mentioned that she didn't get on well with my mother, and she hated my father for the things he'd done to her. She never told me about her life before she came to live with us and I knew better than to ask. Her teenage years were marked by blazing rows with my father that always ended in him beating her severely.

I'd seen him throw her across the room into a wall so hard I'd think she'd been killed. She'd slump on the floor, not moving, seeming impossibly fragile. They argued about her choice of boyfriends, and she actually left home several times but ended up being forced to return because she couldn't make it alone. She'd ended up on the street one time after splitting with the boyfriend she'd been staying with. Dad would forbid us to have contact with her.

One final row broke the cycle and Dad threw Sarina out once and for all. Mum and Dad had had some kind of windfall and took us all on holiday to Spain, leaving Sarina to look after the house. Dad's sister "popped in" to check how Sarina was getting on alone and reported back to my dad that the house was a "complete shit hole", and that Sarina's new boyfriend, Cody, was living there.

Father exploded; he hated Cody, and when we got back home he marched straight round to Cody's house and punched him smack in the face with no warning, knocking him down. Sarina tried to intervene and he hurled her away, spitting that she was disowned and he never wanted to see or hear from her again. He came steaming home and delivered an ultimatum: none of us were allowed to see Sarina from that day on.

As far as I was concerned, Sarina was my sister and I'd see her if I wanted to, so I would visit her and Cody at home or go to the video shop where she worked. I could snatch a quick chat after school or at weekends, and sometimes she took me to see our grandfather – Dad's father – in his electrical shop in town. Eventually Cody and Sarina got married, and obviously there was no question of any of the family being at her wedding.

At the time of my operation, things were starting to go wrong in my relationship with Peter. He'd started to get interested in clubbing, and there was no way I could wrangle a late enough "pass" from my mum to join him. We were drifting apart, but there was no way I would acknowledge that – I had invested so much happiness in Peter and Peter being there for me.

I'd made a special effort for him the day we split up. Usually I wore trousers or jeans, but that day I had a short, cream skirt and knee-length boots that felt really sophisticated and grown up to me. I waited at home at the usual time that Saturday; he'd always pop over to take me back to his parents' house, and my weekends hung on his arrival. I was in my usual state of anticipation, buzzing round and checking my face and hair in the mirror, eager to see him.

Half an hour passed and there was no sign of him. I tried to call him but there was no answer; I reassured myself that he must be on his way, just running a little late. Another half hour passed and he still wasn't there. I thought he must have had an accident, why else wouldn't he have called, at least? I had visions of him lying in the road, being loaded into an ambulance ... I called his home again.

His sister Lisa picked up the phone. She said he wasn't in. I asked if he was on his way over to collect me and she said flatly, "No." I asked if he'd been home at all, because he was supposed to be with me an hour ago. Louise said, "It isn't my place to say. I will tell him you called when he gets in." Then she put the phone down.

I felt like I'd been punched in the stomach. I couldn't breathe, and my heart seemed to have stopped altogether. I'd known, somewhere, that this was coming; I'd had doubts about our relationship for a few weeks. The cute nicknames had stopped and the romance and intensity had been trickling away; it had only been a matter of time. He wanted to dump me. I tried to talk myself out of it, and went back to sit on the sofa and wait. Another hour passed, and another ... My mum asked where Peter was and I told her curtly that I was waiting for him to phone.

Two more hours passed and I was dizzy and nauseous. I decided to try phoning Peter's house again. This time he answered.

"Hi," I said, sheepishly, "I thought you were coming to pick me up this morning."

Peter's voice was emotionless.

"No, I'm not picking you up today. I'm not picking you up any more."

"What? I don't understand!"

"Look, Sam, it's not working out any more. I've met someone else. It's over, I'm sorry."

I was so shocked I could barely take in what he was saying and rang off in silence. I stood in the hall with my mouth hanging open and my hands shaking. I started crying hysterically and couldn't stop, I raced upstairs, desperate to avoid any of my family, I couldn't stand the idea of them asking me any questions. Peter was everything to me; I'd poured all my energy and all my hope into loving him and he'd been my best friend, as well as my boyfriend. I didn't think I could cope without him; if he was gone my family loomed larger than ever and I was utterly alone again.

He'd been a focus for my thoughts and distracted me from what was going on at home. Even though I hadn't dared tell him everything – in case he got scared and backed off – he had known and understood a lot. He was my only outlet; I could cry on his shoulder and be comforted. Unlike the girls who had been my friends at school he never judged and always listened.

I lost control of myself, and all the confidence and security I'd started to build. I felt hollow, and my mind stopped racing and began to fill with one idea – the idea of killing myself. All the wonderful things I'd imagined for us were gone and this time there would be no-one to tell me everything would work out ok in the end. I had to bury my feelings again, when I'd barely begun to open up.

I didn't understand how he could end things so brutally with just one phone call – for me it was as though my entire future had been wiped out because I didn't want to do anything without him now. I resolved that no-one could get that close to me again – I needed my old façade not only to protect me from my family, but also from anyone like Peter who could hurt me like that again.

He'd only been pretending to love me, of course; I'd been right, he couldn't really have been interested in someone like me. I'd probably done everything wrong too – I thought it might be because I wasn't skinny enough or pretty enough. And this new girlfriend must be skinnier and prettier. Who was she anyway? Where did she live and how old was she? How could I have been so stupid to think he'd want to be with me?

I blamed him too, but it was no use as I could do nothing to change his mind; he seemed like a different person now. He'd taken everything and now I didn't think I wanted to love anyone else ever again. It was safer that way. But the best way to be really safe was to put myself beyond pain, and there was one barrier that would defend me from everything – from Peter, from my family, from everyone.

I rushed over to my bed and shoved open the window. I climbed up on to the sill, crying so hard I could barely see the cars passing in the street below. If I jumped it would all be over. I wouldn't have to cope any more, and no-one could touch me. Peter would never forgive himself, I would hurt him as he'd wounded me.

"What are you doing at the window?" That harsh voice – I turned to see my dad standing at the bedroom door. I could barely get a word out, frozen on the sill between suicide and a beating. I just screamed, "I'll jump if you come any closer! Stay away from me!" I half stood up, bent against the window frame, ready to throw myself out. Glancing back I saw him inching towards me. "Don't be so stupid. Whatever it is it can't be that bad. Now come in and tell me what's wrong."

This was such a weird development that I hesitated, and then climbed slowly off the sill and on to my bed, then I just buried my face in my pillow and wept. After a few minutes I told him what had happened in sobs. He sat down the on bed next to me and leant over on to me and prodded a bump under my top. "What's this? Fags?"

I just stared him in the face and said nothing.

"Well, you'd better have one now by the look of things, maybe it'll calm you down a bit, but don't let your mother know." And he got up and walked out, pulling the bedroom door shut behind him. I sat there stunned. My second shock of the day; I'd been sure I'd be in for a thrashing, for smoking at least, but he hadn't even shouted at me. I opened the window again and leaned out to smoke one cigarette after the other and puzzle about the whole thing. I suppose it wasn't exactly a hug, or words of comfort, but it was the closest I'd ever known him to get to being a real dad.

CHAPTER 11

The emotional see-saw

I never heard from Peter again. My father's little show of affection was just a blip and life went back to "normal", though it felt like a big hole had been punched right through me, because now I knew what I was missing out on. No boyfriend, no cosy evenings with Peter's family, and no Sarina either, apart from a few occasions when I could sneak out to see her.

My friendship with Jocelyn was breaking down as we drifted further and further apart; she was more and more on our mother's side, I was just getting increasingly isolated. I was disturbed that only my dad's interruption had stopped me from ending my life at fourteen but I still felt physically sick with the strain of life in that house. I needed to do something, so I fixed up an appointment with my GP.

This involved the same subterfuge as my trip to the family planning clinic because I didn't want anyone else in my family to know how vulnerable I was. I knew they'd tell me I was making it all up and that I had no idea how hard life really was. They'd say I thought I was something special to go running to the doctor. No, I didn't need to confide in anyone at home.

The doctor was and is totally discrete – in fact she treated the whole of my family, so held more of the pieces of the jigsaw than any of us. I knew at that point that my father suffered from depression, but I did not find out till much later that he had been hospitalised a few times and that he made several suicide attempts himself during my early teens. When I was in my twenties I asked around my relatives and found out a few more details. He usually threatened to kill himself when my mum cracked and said she'd leave him, and Mum would pack us kids off to stay with her parents while Dad was in hospital. She never told us, of course, and fed us excuses that we never challenged.

So I suppose my doctor wasn't surprised when I presented myself at the surgery and struggled to describe my symptoms – the fatigue, the hollow hopelessness. I didn't go into any details about home; I just sensed that I needed some kind of cure and that I was incapable of lifting myself out of despair.

She listened carefully and told me gently that she thought I was clinically depressed, which I think I knew, but I couldn't face hearing it. I blurted out that I was scared that that meant I was mad, and I wasn't mad so I couldn't be that sick. My father was the one who was insane, not me. All my life I'd dreaded the idea that one day I'd turn into my father, and here she was telling me we both suffered from the same thing!

I didn't want to be my father's daughter after all the years of struggling against him. I was scared that I'd be carted off and locked up and then everyone would know – my family, Peter, the estate, people at school. Anyway, if Dad was depressed then depression meant being violent and abusive. I thought the doctor was trying to give Dad an excuse for everything he'd done to us, and I started to argue with her.

The doctor smiled and ran over a list of symptoms for depression, which of course fitted me to a T. "You feel exhausted all the time, you have been very low for a long period, you can't concentrate, nothing makes you happy, you feel worthless. And you tried to kill yourself." She took time to explain that depression did not necessarily mean psychosis, and that I wasn't "mad", but ill – physically ill, in a way. "Your brain is filled with nerve cells called neurons which receive and transmit messages around your body – thoughts, actions. They use chemicals called neurotransmitters to pass these messages on." She showed me a diagram of neurons, which looked like a cable with a break in them, and the neurotransmitters, which travelled across the gap in the cable.

"When you are depressed the neurotransmitters don't function very well and your brain gets confused and slows down. I can prescribe you drugs that will boost the neurotransmitters, but you should have counselling too. Depression is an illness which has physical effects but you need to be able to cope with it emotionally too, because that's where you feel it."

The idea of being able to take a pill, something I could hide under my mattress away from prying parents and siblings, and getting better was perfect, but I shied away from counselling. Arranging the appointments would require more sneaking around and snatching time between school and curfew, and I didn't want to talk about things. I thought keeping quiet was the only tactic that had saved me so far. I didn't know what would happen if I opened that Pandora's Box.

So I backed off, but took my prescription for 20mg of Seroxat, once daily, and my doctor reassured me that she would monitor me closely and if I had any problems with the drug she'd let me come off it and try a different one, "There are lots of different types, and it might just be that one suits you more than another." I felt doubtful but I took the tablets.

The GP had warned that I might feel nauseous for the first few weeks, and I did feel queasy all the time, but it lasted more than a month. It slowed me down even more, and I was moving through the motions of life – home, school, home, chores, bed – in a sick daze. My hands developed a tremor too and I got even more irritable with everyone around me. Despite this, my mood had lifted a bit, so I decided to get rid of the medication and shed the side effects too. I stopped taking it abruptly after three months and suffered crushing headaches. I later learned you should take antidepressants for six months to give them a chance to work, and you should never stop taking them abruptly, but I was too impatient.

This was the beginning of a cycle which repeated itself throughout my teenage years. I would become depressed to the point of suicide, then be prescribed drugs, take them for a short time then throw away the packet. Sometimes I got sick of the side effects and sometimes I found a new "solution" – my first three-month stint on Seroxat ended when I met my second boyfriend, Graham, and I went into an ecstatic up-swing again.

If I was in love I believed I was fine and I didn't need the tablets. I based all my happiness on my boyfriends and built no confidence up for myself. I was either "high" and dependent on the boyfriend, or low and desolate. At best I was papering over my problems either with medication or relationships that were bound to fail.

I had just met someone who would change my life in the end though, but of course I didn't know it at the time. It wasn't a new boyfriend, though Graham made a lot of things much more bearable for me. It was our new next-door neighbour.

We moved house when I was still in my wheelchair and before I had split with Peter. The new place was a three-bedroom semi because my parents had somehow scraped together enough cash for a mortgage. It was three storeys high, and in a far better state than the old council house, but it was right next to a busy road where cars sped past day and night. I should have been back at school but because of the operation I was still home for a few weeks.

My parents were busy ferrying our stuff over in car loads from the old house and had left me on my own on the top floor. I was gasping for a cigarette, so hobbled down the stairs on my crutches and, with difficulty, hefted the wheelchair out the back door. Climbing in I wheeled myself laboriously down the garden and negotiated the gate to let myself into the little park behind the row of houses. I sparked up a cigarette and felt shattered. At least I knew Mum and Dad would be gone for long enough for me to smoke it.

I heard a deep, chesty cough beside me and looked round to see a man standing next to me with a cigarette in the corner of his mouth. He was tallish with a generous belly and wiry, messy hair which stuck up in places. He reminded me a bit of Wurzel Gummidge and his expression was very open and kind. He had an amused, gentle voice when he smiled and asked me, "Are you old enough to be smoking?"

"No, and don't tell my parents you caught me or they'll kill me." Panic rose in my chest.

"I promise I won't say a word. My name's Geoff, by the way, and you must be my new neighbour."

I introduced myself in turn and he told me a little about himself. I found myself warming to him and slowly relaxing because he seemed quite happy to chat to me and pass the time. I realised I could trust him not to tell my parents about the cigarette. He was married to Mandy and they had two young children, Kieley and Scott; they'd all been living there for a few years and he worked as a gas man. I mentioned that it was my birthday and he wished me happy birthday and asked what I was doing to celebrate.

I must have looked nonplussed. "I had a card from my sisters and brother and a card from my mum and she says I've got to wait till she has money for my present." We never had cakes or parties in our family – and that was just the way things were. It was Geoff's turn to look puzzled; he took a few more puffs on his fag and shook his head, "Well, that's terrible, I'm sorry to hear that."

Then he quickly changed the subject and, head on one side, asked me why I was in a wheelchair. I explained about the operation and he told me he'd wondered if I was paralysed at first, and that if so it was odd that my family had moved into such a tall, narrow house. I smiled and said, "Well, it's just as well I'm not paralysed then, isn't it?" and he chuckled. That was how I met the man who saved my life, but that was all a long time in the future.

Life in the new house was pretty much the same as on the council estate. Dad installed his security cameras again and the speakers too. He had one in the garage that eavesdropped on the kitchen, so that even when he was working he could keep one ear on what was going on in the house. He also wired up a microphone in the room I shared with Jocelyn and Charmaine and a bell, so we could be summoned by my mum without her having to go all the way upstairs to the top floor.

Shortly after he did this I climbed up on a chair and stuck a knife in the speaker. I waggled it around and somehow broke the circuitry, and it never worked after that. He can't have realised because he never mended it – I expect he thought we'd finally learned our lesson and didn't talk after lights out any more! The bell was annoying though, especially if we were all asleep and Mum only wanted one of us.

CHAPTER 12

A normal life

When I had a boyfriend or whenever I gained an inch or two more freedom – a later curfew, for example – I could start to become something different. Not even my parents could stop us all from growing into adults. I could do a little more, say a little more, behave a little more like myself and try and build my own personality. I would start to imagine what life would be like when I was a young woman and when I would finally break away and be free once and for all. I needed to totally disassociate myself from my parents so no-one would ever judge me because of the things they did.

I couldn't help being born into that family, but I could gradually sever all the ties that bound us together. I not only buried my feelings, but also killed some of them off altogether, cutting my way out of their destructive web. So I didn't care any more that I had hit my own mother. I wouldn't try to make my father like me any more. However much they nagged or cursed me, or even beat me, they couldn't change what I thought inside.

I had passed a hurdle, I had shredded more pain. I knew that if I maintained my new found strength, my thoughts, my choices; they couldn't touch me. I stayed out of conversations and sat in silence rather than draw attention to myself. Sometimes getting involved was unavoidable, and that usually ended in big rows, but on the whole I kept out of it altogether. I didn't have to agree with them, I didn't have to behave like they insisted I did, especially when I wasn't around them. I was a person after all, not a dog that needed obedience training. If I could help it, they would never see me vulnerable again.

I fought every day to be different so I wouldn't become my father − bitter, twisted, miserable and unapproachable − or my mother − weak and dependent. So I'd smile at passersby, because I wanted them to find me friendly and judge me on my own merits. I would only tell people what they needed to know and wouldn't elaborate any further, so they wouldn't have any ammunition to use against me as I trusted barely anyone.

In my mind's eye I saw no colour − everything was right or wrong, black or white, yes or no, odd or even. Compromise wasn't something that I knew about, understood or could even attempt to have in my life. It never rained, it poured. When something went wrong, I had to be able to deal with it, I had to be able to fix it or forget about it, and then move on pretending like nothing had happened.

A few months after Peter and I split up, when I was trying to handle the side effects of the Seroxat, I met another biker. I was walking along the pavement to the garage and someone on a motorbike passed, turning back to look at me as he went. I always looked closely at people on motorbikes in case one of them happened to be Peter on a new bike. By the time I got to the garage the biker and a friend had pulled up at the pumps.

He took off his crash helmet and I instantly recognised him. He'd been two years above me at the same secondary school as me. I walked over and we got talking. His friend hadn't said anything or even flipped up his visor so I asked him to remove his helmet. After some deliberation he reluctantly pulled it off and said apologetically that he hadn't had much time to do his hair. I smiled and said I didn't mind at all, and he introduced himself as Graham.

We started dating almost immediately, and he only lived five minutes walk from me. He was three years older and worked as an apprentice at a machine factory. He'd been to my school too. I took the usual precaution of introducing him to my parents and briefing him on what to expect. Mum was perfectly polite but somewhat withdrawn. Dad, astonishingly, shook his hand and sat down with him in the living room for a spot of polite conversation, which baffled Graham who must have been expecting the third degree.

Graham's parents were great to me. I used to rush home from school, get changed, do my homework, bolt my dinner and do my chores then run all the way to Graham's house every evening to see him. His mum would invite me to join them for supper and we'd all sit down together in front of EastEnders. She was a lovely cook and I was always so famished after a scant, burnt meal at home that I relished the chance to feel full for once. When it was my birthday she even bought me a cake and I burst into tears because it was such a kind gesture. Graham's family were convinced they'd done something wrong and upset me!

After we'd eaten Graham and I would disappear to his room together and lie in one another's arms for an hour or so before I had to go home and meet my curfew. He'd walk me back and kiss me goodnight at the gate, gutted that I couldn't stay out with him. He never let my parents' strictness ruin our relationship though.

One night when Graham was saying goodnight, Geoff was out in his front garden having a last cigarette. I introduced them to each other and we chatted, then Geoff, probably being mindful of the fact we wanted to be alone for a little, toddled back indoors.

"You know who he reminds me of, Sam?" said Graham.

"Yes, I do," I said with a cheeky grin on my face, "He reminds you of Worzel Gummidge, doesn't he?" I laughed.

"Spot on!" Our affectionate nickname for Geoff from that moment on was "Gummidge".

If his mum hadn't been home to cook dinner and he'd delivered me home still hungry, Graham would nip off to KFC on his motorbike, pick me up a zinger burger and drive past the house beeping his horn. After waiting for a minute or two to look less conspicuous, I'd go upstairs to our room on the top floor.

I'd open the window to see him standing by his bike, beaming from ear to ear, a bag in his hand. I'd tie a bottle of water to a sheet and lower it out of the window, praying it wouldn't knock on the living room window as it went past. He'd tie the bag of KFC to the sheet and I'd hoist it back up carefully. He'd have written a little letter too, for me to read as I ate my burger. Any drivers passing by would have wondered what on earth was happening, but we didn't care!

We had a shared joke about Peter Rabbit and he'd draw pictures of him on the letters, telling him to stay away from me as I was his bird! It had all come about because one day we had been in Graham's garden when he'd wanted a cigarette. His parents didn't know he smoked so we thought we'd pop over the back fence into a farmer's field to hide. I picked up a stone and threw it into the field as far as I could and shouted, "Take that, Peter!" Later Graham told me that when I turned back to him and smiled it was the first moment he realised that he was in love with me.

I was blissfully happy again now that I had him, and I stopped taking the antidepressants abruptly, which wasn't very sensible. I thought I'd never need them again, Graham and I were having so much fun. I broke into a more adult world of pubs and nightclubs, though I never dared drink much and was anxious if I was left alone. Graham knew that and stuck close to me to be sure I was ok.

I wasn't supposed to ride on his motorbike as Father had told me they were too dangerous, and then threatened that if I went behind his back and got on one, it'd be the last thing I did. He didn't seem to see the contradiction in backing up his "protectiveness" with death threats! I was so happy being with Graham and desperate not to miss out on anything that I defied him anyway and we'd go off to Chelsea Bridge in London on a Friday night to meet up with other bikers. Then we could sit and watch everyone doing stunts up and down the bridge before speeding home to meet my curfew.

Sometimes he got frustrated with my parents because of their strictness but I was grateful that he didn't let it complicate things. I didn't tell him much about life with them; if he asked a question I'd answer it, if I wanted to share that detail. He usually said that they "seemed alright" to him or that he "couldn't see it" himself, so I didn't push the issue. Years later they invited him round to dinner, which was typically two-faced of Mother and Father. They'd caused all kinds of problems when we were dating but later they were anxious to make a good impression.

I asked Graham if he was going to go, and he said he'd told them he'd think about it but had no intention of going as he didn't want to hurt my feelings. He was so decent to me and trusting that, even years after we'd split up, he respected me like that, even though he doubted that my family was all that bad.

The one time I do remember him getting angry with them was on my sixteenth birthday. He'd planned to take me into town to treat me to a present, but my parents wouldn't let me go out. They were so strapped for cash that they'd got some work to do at home, boxing up greetings cards for a manufacturer. It didn't pay well, so they were determined to rope all of us in to get through piles and piles of boxes. We weren't even allowed out before the curfew because there was so much to be done. If we knew what was good for us we'd get stuck in.

This had begun months before my birthday and at first Graham offered to help, but the novelty soon wore off. By the time my birthday came round and we were still labouring away he was furious.

There was nothing either of us could do about the situation. Although I treasured Graham, I was still hurt by what had happened with Peter and I reasoned to myself that I couldn't afford to get too close to him. After all, he might take off with someone else, and I'd be desolate again. I could never really let myself go and really love him, which was a great shame.

CHAPTER 13

The photo session

It was around this time, but before my exams that a particularly worrying incident took place at home. I was still haunted by what Sarina had told me about her experience with my father years ago, and sharing a house with him made me feel really claustrophobic. The way he'd sometimes pounce out of the bathroom and grope my breasts when I was waiting in the corridor had been disturbing enough, but this was worse.

After Sarina's confidences I developed a lingering sense of danger which was nothing to do with being violently beaten. It weighed heavily on me, and I felt that because I had these fears it was my responsibility to protect my sisters and brother. Mother was working nights at a residential home, where Dad would drop her off at 10pm every evening. When she left she'd tell us to go to bed when he told us to, and my father would stand behind her, fag in one hand, car keys clunking in the other. Then he'd come back and settle down in the living room in front of the telly.

I just knew that my father should never be left alone with any of the others. However tired I was I could not go to bed myself until they had got safely out of his way. If I was out babysitting for my aunt I would sit in her house fretting about what was happening at home, and whether they were tucked up alright. Perhaps it was just the result of the strain of our day-to-day existence under Dad's thumb, or maybe I was absolutely right to be so afraid. I just thought it was my job to see that nothing happened to them.

I was about fifteen when my dad came home one day with a handful of bits of lingerie and asked me if I would pose for photographs for him, saying, "You still want to do some modelling, don't you Samantha?" A few days beforehand an ex work colleague of his had been round with a folder of glamour shots of women dolled up in suspenders and bras and stockings. Father used to slag this guy off behind his back, but the two of them buddied up on the sofa to ogle the pictures, commenting loudly on each woman's "assets". I'd left the room in disgust.

They'd obviously had a great brainwave in the meantime and decided to persuade us girls – my father's own daughters – to strip off so they could try their hand at being soft porn barons. Dad said he'd take the pictures himself at home and I'd be paid for them. I didn't know what would happen if I refused; it wasn't as if Dad had taken no for an answer in the past. His methods of persuasion weren't exactly gentle either. I was scared that he might ask Charmaine to do it instead, and that she'd have even less idea of what she was getting herself into than I did. So I reluctantly agreed.

He spent the next few nights creating a kind of studio in the living room, moving the dining table and rigging up lighting and a backdrop made of a white bed sheet. When this was done I had to get changed into the underwear and stand in front of his camera pretty much naked while he gave me directions: "Move your arm, open your legs more, stick your tits out!" I moved stiffly from position to position, feeling cold and exposed.

I tried to remove myself mentally from what was going on and make it through, no matter how hideously wrong it all was. Dad clicked away, only concerned with getting the right shot; it was more degrading than anything I'd ever experienced, and I couldn't fight my rising disgust when he said I should take my bra off so he could get, "some tasteful topless shots, like in the *Sun*".

At that point, thank God, I found the courage to blurt out "no", and miraculously he left it at that. In due course the photos were developed and stored in their own folder. I was paid the princely sum of twenty pounds for being humiliated and I never found out what he did with the pictures.

CHAPTER 14

Love vs. Prozac

Despite Graham's presence my depression started to creep back after a while and I was back in trouble. I was supposed to be doing my GCSEs but concentration seemed impossible, and I was withdrawing from what little social life I had. I went back on antidepressants, still refusing counselling, but I didn't think the pills were working. Now I know that there is only so much that drugs can do, and they didn't exactly solve my difficulties at home, but then I just thought I needed to take something different.

After another suicide attempt my GP switched me to Prozac which gave me fewer side effects. It saw me through my exams, and I did very well, getting the results I needed to go on to the sixth form – 4 Cs and a B. I wanted a better life than my parents' and further education was the first step towards that. A good education would give me a firmer foundation than they had ever bothered to get. So, delighted with my exam results and excited about starting college, I came off the Prozac overnight and again suffered the consequences. I met someone new almost immediately though, and that was enough for me.

I'd enrolled on a business studies course and was busy making the most of my lectures. One day after a class another student came over for a chat and casually told me that his brother really liked me. As we talked I realised who he was talking about – a gorgeous-looking guy I'd seen once before and remembered well. It had been a few days earlier when I'd popped out during my lunchbreak to see Graham. A large van was driving towards me on the road and I mistook it for a neighbour, so smiled and waved. As soon as it had passed, I realised I'd been wrong, but the driver seemed very nice anyway.

A short time later my fellow student invited me round to his house, and because I'd guessed that his good-looking brother would be there I took a friend for support. Sure enough Stewart just happened to show up and we hit it off really well. I was bowled over; here was a handsome, charming man who was twelve years older than me. He was so grown up – he had his own car, his own home. He worked out five times a week and I just thought he was the best looking man in town.

All my old fears rose up – the nagging idea that such a catch of a bloke could never be interested in me, or want to know about my shitty life – but Stewart was confident and just the thought of him sent shivers up my spine. I didn't start dating him immediately, but my feelings for Graham started to cool and I found myself spending less time with him and more time thinking of Stewart. The contrast between the way I felt about the two of them made me realise that my heart hadn't been in my relationship with Graham for a long time.

Graham hadn't guessed, and one night after a lot of soul searching I just came out and said that I thought we should split up. Graham was heartbroken and I hated having to hurt him but it seemed like it was the only thing to do. Later he found out that I had fallen for Stewart and that had triggered my decision and was furious because he thought I'd been cheating on him for months. It wasn't true though, because I'd been careful to make the break with him before I began dating Stewart.

I was totally besotted with my new boyfriend, even more I think than I was with Peter. I'd have done anything to make him happy, but the flipside of that devotion was a fear that he'd leave me one day. The age gap between us created lots of problems, or at least it worried our friends and relatives and they put pressure on us in turn.

My parents didn't like it one bit, but by that time Jocelyn had begun seeing someone who was six years older than her and I think Dad probably found Stewart with his gym body physically intimidating. Father had started to withdraw into a very serious bout of depression and didn't have the energy to care about what us kids did. We still had our curfew, but he was less vigilant and touchy so we were a bit more free to do as we liked.

Some of my friends' parents thought I'd end up being a bad influence on their daughters by "hanging around pubs with older men" but when they actually met

Stewart they were won over because he was so genuine. His mates gave him some stick and his mum really disapproved and didn't want to invite me to family gatherings, which didn't help. I think she knew some things about my background and was wary about what I might do to her son.

Stewart would reassure me that he loved me and that was all that mattered, but my fears could make me difficult. I knew I was in deep, so I felt like I had to be ready to defend myself all the time. If a female friend called him I'd give Stewart the third degree. Who was she? How did he know her? Why had she phoned? He'd try to explain and I'd have difficulty trusting him, I was getting so paranoid. This led to arguments and they took their toll on both of us.

He kept trying to prove how much he cared but I was haunted by the idea that he'd leave me for someone older that he had more in common with. He'd done so much and I thought he'd find me and my life boring because with me he'd only be going back over things he'd already experienced for himself. I was prepared to sacrifice my own future plans of seeing the world if it meant I could keep Stewart with me by settling down with him and having kids – something he was close to wanting at his age. If I had chosen that path I know now I would have been unhappy and resentful towards him.

Of course we were good together too when I was feeling safe and all was right in the world. We spent hours riding around the countryside on his motorbike –

a Z11 Chopper. The suspension wasn't much cop so I was relieved when he traded it in for a Ducati Monster which was more like the type of bike his friends rode. It was sportier and better for stunts and he poured plenty of time and effort into making it look really great by readapting the faring and painting the wheels gold. I loved that bike and was proud of it and my boyfriend.

As he learned how to handle the bike better I got more and more confident about riding with him but one day we had an accident that put paid to my career as a pillion passenger. We were bowling back from an outing one boiling hot afternoon when all of a sudden a little boy on a bike shot out on to the road from between two parked cars. We couldn't swerve to avoid him because there was a car speeding towards us on the other side of the road.

Stewart flipped the bike on its side and we skidded down the road with it, our legs trapped underneath against the road. We came to an abrupt halt at the feet of the little boy, who toppled over on to us still on his bike. The Ducati's throttle was buried in the hot tarmac leaving a long scar the length of our skid.

Stewart freed himself from the wreckage first and quickly got the boy and his bike onto the pavement. A passerby helped me out from under the bike and Stewart wheeled the Ducati to the side of the road. The little boy just jumped on his cycle and shot off without saying a word. I'd only been wearing jeans and had a big friction burn on the side of my knee where I'd been scraped along the tarmac.

I never got back on a motorbike again after that. I made sure my parents never found out because I still wasn't allowed to go near one of the things in the first place, and I hid the injury carefully. It took a while to heal too. They might not even have taken the trouble to ground me by that stage though, because things at home were getting steadily worse.

CHAPTER 15

Breaking away

Dad's depression was deepening fast, and he'd largely given up work in favour of sitting around in the living room watching the telly. He made some cash working as a courier, but not much. Jocelyn had left school and got a job by that stage, but her wages weren't enough to make up the shortfall left by Dad. She was starting to resent me for still being a student, even though it had been her choice to quit. Mum was working nights at the residential home and doing day shifts as a lollipop lady and worker in a school canteen. She was exhausted and even more aggressive and tetchy than usual.

Mum and Dad started to put pressure on me to leave sixth form and start work so I could contribute to the mortgage. I'd hoped that if I could just stay on a while longer and get my qualifications I'd get an even better job. I'd done a year – half the course – and I didn't want to throw it all away.

They began to wear me down. Mum would make a point of telling me just how bad the financial situation was, and just how far in arrears the mortgage payments had gone. She was always on the scrounge for any spare cash I had. Jocelyn guilt-tripped me, telling me she didn't see why I should have the luxury of further education when she worked.

Although I was trying to distance myself emotionally from them all, there was no way I could have just upped and left home then. I still believed like my dad had told me time and time again, that I wouldn't be able to cope on my own. I did feel responsible for my siblings though, and I began to feel guilty too. I knew there was no point in arguing, and that my father wasn't going to suddenly get up off the couch and start functioning like a normal human being. I took their word for it and eventually I caved in; they made it sound as though my selfishness would leave them all on the street.

I told my college I wouldn't be coming back in the autumn and drafted a CV. Nobody thanked me. Giving up my education wasn't seen as a sacrifice but as something I just should have done anyway. As I said before, my parents didn't want better things for us kids; and my sisters and brother didn't seem to see why I'd want to improve my life either. They barely acknowledged what had happened. In our family you were just supposed to endure everything and think yourself lucky.

I went to the job centre with my mother. I filled out several forms and had a chat with the woman in reception about the type of jobs I could do. She suggested a local recruitment agency and an IT company who were currently looking for a receptionist who'd do admin too, so I applied for both jobs.

I got the post with the recruitment agency and knuckled down to work. For a few months, things at home improved. As soon as payday came round I'd have to withdraw everything from the bank in cash and hand it over to my mother for the bills. I'd never had so much money before and I was working hard for it but there was no chance of me being rewarded with some pocket money for a spending spree in town. If I wanted to have my sisters and brother fed, clothed and keep them off the streets, I had no choice. It made no real difference to my curfew either – in the eyes of my parents I still wasn't an adult even if I was keeping them from bankruptcy.

After a year of nine-to-five at the recruitment agency, the usual chores and black moods at home and snatched time with Stewart, I heard from the IT company again. They wanted to know if I was interested in working for them. I seized the opportunity and was ecstatic when I discovered I'd be earning a few thousand pounds more every year. I told my parents I'd secured a bit more cash, but kept most of the extra to myself as I was desperate to have something of a life. I bought myself a pet too, a chinchilla called Alby.

I hadn't been in my new job long when one day I received a call from my mother at work. She seemed to be totally hysterical and at first I could hardly make out a word she was saying; I transferred the call to another room so I could take it privately, trying to reassure her and calm her. She slowed down a little but her tone was still frantic. "It's your dad, Sam," she sniffed, "He's at home and he won't let anyone in the house."

"What are you going on about? You've lost me."

"I told him I was going to leave him; before I went to work, last night," she was shouting madly down the phone at me now, "So he came to the residential home last night and told me he was going to commit suicide!"

I'd had no idea that things at home had come to such a head, but something snapped in me and I lost all my professionalism and forgot I was in the office.

"Oh, for fuck's sake! What's his fucking problem? Why does he always use that line when you say that to him?" I was furious with him, with her. Why did she fall for his emotional blackmail? Why did she think she owed him anything given the way he treated us all?

Mum started crying again, her voice arching up squeakily as she tried to tell me something more.

"So what happened after he said that, then?" I felt sceptical but I needed to know what was going on.

"I told him not to be so stupid," she let out a sob, "Next thing you know he's just driven off down the road like a lunatic in the courier van."

I wasn't too surprised to hear that because he'd threatened to write off several cars before.

"Why didn't you go after him?"

"You know what he's like, Sam. He would probably have thumped me or something, besides, I couldn't leave work. I was the only member of staff there."

I could picture the scene, Dad roaring off in the van in a trance-like state, foot forcing the accelerator to the floor, pointing the van at something, a tree, a wall, another car …

"So what's happened since then?"

"I tried to call him all night but there's no answer, no-one's picking up the phone. I got a taxi home this morning but he's barricaded the door and I can't get in. He's done something, Sam. You can see the state of the kitchen through the window. He's ransacked the place. I think he's dead. I really think he's done it this time. I've called the police. I'm at Auntie Jane's at the moment but they're going to come to your office and get your keys. Will you go with them and see what's going on?"

I struggled to take in what she'd just said, heart in my mouth. My manager and some other colleagues were standing in the doorway, and must have heard the way the conversation was going and guessed that something serious had happened. I clutched the receiver. My manager mouthed "are you ok?" and I shook my head and turned back to face the wall, staring straight through it. I was scared, but now I became angry. I told my mum I'd sort things out with the police and call her back. I put the phone down.

"My dad may have committed suicide," I blurted out. I started to cry with pure rage; how could my parents do this? I'd only been in the job for a few weeks and nobody there knew about my homelife. I was trying so damn hard to be normal and to do well and to be my own person, and now my family had ruined it all. I'd grown up with a kind of unspoken family code that nobody outside the house found out about what was going on. Now that was blown to the wind.

"The police are on their way here to pick me up and take me home. They need my keys to get into the house. They may find him dead, I just don't know."

My manager looked horrified, but I didn't know how I should feel; I was just stunned. What else could I have said? I was tired of home, the arguments and the menacing tension of living with my father. I didn't care what happened to him any more. I was fed up with being the one that everyone in the family relied on to solve all the problems. I hoped he had really done it this time and it would all be over; then we would all be free.

My manager walked over to me and I just threw myself into his arms and cried even harder, stuttering that I was sorry again and again.

"Please don't apologise Sam, it's not your fault. Is … is there anything we can do?"

I shook my head, tears streaming.

"Fucking hell, Sam … I can't believe this … shit … what the fuck?"

He sat with me as I smoked my way through several cigarettes. When the policeman arrived he didn't need to ask who I was, my face gave it away. I simply handed him the keys and told him I had no intention of going to the house with him. He nodded, smiled reassuringly and said he would organise someone to get in touch and keep me informed.

I needed to talk to Stewart and quickly dialled his number, realising with a sinking heart that now he would have to know everything that I'd tried to hide from him about my family.

"Hi!" he answered chirpily, pleased to get a call from me.

"Stewart, it's me … Look, something's happened, where are you?"

"I'm at William and Katrina's. What's up? Are you ok? What's wrong?" William and Katrina were our other next-door neighbours; Stewart had a ringside seat for Dad's suicide attempt. I told him between sobs what was going on, and he raced upstairs, holding the phone to watch the scene unfold from a bedroom window. I don't think he took me seriously at first, and I reckon he thought he'd indulge me, but then his voice changed.

"Holy shit, Sam! There's swarms of pigs out the back of your house. There's police dogs and a riot van! What the fuck?"

"Please Stewart, just stay on the phone and tell me what's happening."

"OK, hang on a sec though, I need to tell William."

He put his hand over the receiver but I could still hear him relaying everything to William, and William's muffled response. He didn't seem to believe what was going on either. Stewart spoke to me again, demanding answers.

"What's provoked this? What's going on? Where is he? Where's your mum? Has he done this before?"

I was too distraught to start explaining everything now and begged him to just tell me what the hell was going on.

"They are banging on the back door and calling his name … Now they're kicking it down. There's about six officers standing around and two working on the door. He must have barricaded it … Now they're in … Hang on …"

The office was very quiet and still around me.

"They are shouting, banging around … hang on …" The phone cut out. I hit redial and Stewart picked up immediately, "Wait a second … Hang on a minute … There's loads of screaming."

"What's going on? What can you hear? Stewart!" I could hear some of the shouting down the phone.

"Oh, my God. Get away from the window, William. William, listen …"

"Stewart, tell me what's happening."

"The police are shouting at him to put down the knife. He's gotta be in the bathroom 'cause we can hear them through the walls."

"Is he saying anything?"

"I can't hear. Oh, hang on." He broke off. "William's just told me that more officers have just gone in the back door with protective vests on."

"I'm coming round!" I couldn't stand just listening to this any more. I needed to be there and see for myself what was happening. I'd lost any idea of where I was and had screamed down the phone at Stewart and now the whole office was disturbed.

"You can't come here," said Stewart, "The police have cordoned off the road and they aren't letting anyone past. There's an ambulance out there as well."

I slammed the phone down on him and told my manager I had to get home, *now*. After the initial numbness, I could feel my adrenalin pumping fiercely and when he tried to say I shouldn't go alone, I brought him up sharp. He wouldn't want to be there, and he shouldn't get involved. I'd be fine. I'd call him. I took my bag and headed out of the door at a run, leaving everyone gawping after me.

Home was only a couple of minutes away, and as I turned the corner into our street I could see a mass of people outside my house. There were two riot vans, policemen everywhere, in Kevlar vests, with Alsatians; there was the ambulance and cameramen – reporters! I saw my father then, strapped into a straitjacket, being half carried by four policemen through the crowd and manhandled into the back of a van.

They slammed the van door behind him, and the vehicle started up and headed off to God knows where. He was gone. Everyone started to melt away, leaving me and a few curious neighbours standing in the road. Stewart came out of William and Katrina's house, craning his head right and left till he spotted me. He rushed over and I buried myself in his arms, trying to blot out everything I'd just seen.

After a while he said softly, "Your mum's indoors."

I pulled myself away reluctantly and began to trudge to our front gate, which I opened with trembling hands, punchdrunk with shock. Stewart trailed behind me into the kitchen, where Mum was standing talking to a handful of police officers. I walked straight past them all up to my bedroom. I would not take a second more of this. My family would have to get along without me to hit or threaten. I wanted to leave, and I was going to leave now.

I ripped my clothes from their hangers and stuffed them frantically into plastic bags. I took handfuls of underwear and socks and crammed them in, then turned to Stewart who was standing in the doorway, watching me in horror.

"I want you to carry Alby out of the house and put him in your car." I demanded. Without a word he picked up the cage and followed me back down stairs to the dining room where my mother's brother-in-law was lurching around, drunk out of his skull. He was shaking his head and muttering that my dad was a wanker, "Cccan't believe 'ees done this again", he slurred. I let rip:

"Oh shut up you *fucking* piss-head! Look at the state of you! Who asked you to come round here anyway? Piss off back home. You're no use to anyone in that state."

He was stunned and just stared vaguely at me as I took a last look around the room. Father had wrecked the place. There were pills and empty boxes all over the floor; paper was confettied everywhere and all the plates smashed. Whatever damage he'd managed to do to himself with the knife, he'd also had a try at an overdose too. I went into the kitchen.

The policemen had gone and Mum was now standing by the sideboard talking to another woman. Ignoring them, my eye fell on a letter sitting on one of the stools. On the front of it was written "My Angel" in my father's handwriting. This had to be his suicide note. Once when I was little I'd found some love letters my dad had sent my mum, and he'd called her "Angel" then.

I snatched it up and ripped it open, scanning it rapidly. Dad didn't write much but when he did his writing was immaculate. It read something like this:

To my Angel,
I am sorry for everything I have ever put you and the children through. I honestly never did any of it intentionally and I hope that one day you will find it in your hearts to forgive me. I want you to be happy, I want our children to be happy, I think you will all be better off without me and so I am saying my last goodbye. I hope that our children, Jocelyn, Samantha, Charmaine and Jacob, will live long and happy lives. I want them to marry well and have loving relationships and children that love them dearly …

I couldn't read any more. My jaw was clenched and the muscles of my back were knotted in a rictus. I screwed up the letter into a ball and hurled across the room screaming,

"He's a lying, cheating, conniving wanker and he deserves to rot in hell for everything he's put us through! I want him *dead*! Why couldn't he get it right the fucking first time?" There was no holding me now I'd started to pour out all these things that I'd been bottling up for so long. I was hysterical, but I felt every word I said.

Stewart was behind me, still silent, but Alby had woken up and was jumping around his cage in a panic. Mum just stared at me, then colour flooded her face and she began to yell back at me.

"He's your father!"

"I didn't choose him!"

She moved fast, slamming me back into the wall, her hand on my throat. Pinning me there she bellowed right into my face, "He is your FATHER!"

"No, he's not! Not any more. I've had it. I hope he DIES and if he ever comes anywhere near me again I'll put a knife in him myself! I'll make sure I do the job PROPERLY with my own bare hands!"

The other woman wrestled my mum off me, but she didn't let up.

"Get out of my house! I never want to see your face again!"

"GOOD! I've had it. I'm sick of all this bullshit. I should have grassed him up long ago."

My uncle wandered in at this point to see what all the fuss was about, and when he saw my mum, who was in a worse state by far than me, he helped pinion her arms. The other woman must have been some kind of

Social Services representative, and was trying to talk to Stewart, but he squeezed out of the kitchen to his car. I couldn't be bothered with her and turned to leave forever, when she stepped in front of me and said in an oh-so-concerned, delicate voice, "And how are you feeling, Samantha?"

This was the icing on the cake; I roared, "What the fuck do you think I'm feeling, you silly cow?" then pushed past her with my two carrier bags.

Stewart had loaded Alby into the boot of his car and opened the front doors. "What are we doing?" he asked as we climbed in.

"We are going back to your house." My voice had now fallen to a flat monotone, but was still seething with fury.

"But we can't just leave them here. We should at least take them back to your aunt's."

I caved in; we could do that, but I wouldn't stand for anything more. I walked back into the house and told Mum what would happen. Charmaine, Jocelyn and Jacob had appeared and were sitting on the sofa looking bootfaced. I think they must have been there when Mum and I were fighting in the kitchen. Jocelyn was trying to comfort the two younger ones, who were all of sixteen and fifteen.

Mum barely said a word as they all squeezed into the back of Stewart's car, but as we drove to my aunt's house they began to fight with one another and I piled in when my mother started at me again. Everyone was upset, but of course, in my family, nobody comforted anyone, so the only way we knew of dealing with what had happened was to attack each other. Mum changed her tune, "I'm leaving him. I'm not going back this time. We're all going to be evicted now."

"Just shut up, the lot of you!" I shouted back. I didn't want Charmaine and Jacob to get any more scared. They all fell silent.

When we reached my aunt's house my mum hauled them all out of the car with their little bags of hastily packed clothes. I didn't move. I couldn't face being anywhere near them as they bickered and moaned with each other. My mum had other ideas.

She bent down to the car window, "Come on, Samantha."

"Oh, I'm not going anywhere with you lot."

"Don't be stupid. Get out of the car."

"Fuck off! I'm eighteen years old and I can do what the hell I like and I'm NOT coming with you lot."

Stewart put his hand gently on my leg, "Go on, Sam. You're probably better off with your family."

"NO WAY! Get lost; I'm not moving from this car. I'm going back with you." I knew Stewart was really unhappy with the situation, but I couldn't budge. He'd have to deal with it. He drove me back to his house, leaving Mum and my siblings on the pavement. We didn't speak throughout the whole journey. I think neither of us wanted to risk saying anything in case the other flew off the handle. I didn't need to know if

Stewart was having second thoughts, I'd had enough to cope with already. He might not want to be with me any more now that he knew the truth about my family, and I couldn't face that. I had just cut myself off from them all, for better or for worse, and I had no-one but Stewart in the world.

His mind must have been racing to try and understand everything that had happened and fit it together with all the things I had told him over the past few years. Now he knew I had never lied or exaggerated about what was going on. He'd seen it all first hand. He must be thinking about how much I needed him now and how serious the implications were.

When we walked in his front door he walked straight over to the drinks cabinet and took out a bottle of whisky.

"Want a drink?"

"Yes please," I said quietly. I thought he couldn't keep quiet much longer and that he must be furious with me. I expected him to explode any minute, and throw me out of the house. He gave me a glass with a generous shot in it and we sat side by side on the sofa. I sipped at mine, and he downed his in one swig. I started, tentatively, "If Dad gets out he'll come and find me. He'll want to know where everyone is. He knows where you live. He'll try something."

"You really reckon he'd come round?"

"I just don't know. He's capable of anything."

We spent the whole night there in the living room, wide awake. Whenever we heard someone talking outside we'd start. When car headlights flooded the room we'd edge to the window and peer round the curtain, scanning the street. I was tortured by the thought of my father out there, screaming and ranting, and what he might do to me.

He never came.

CHAPTER 16

No turning back

The next morning I barely knew what to do with myself. Stewart and I still hadn't talked about whether I could stay at his house or not, and I had nowhere else to stay. The events of the day before were running through my mind like an endless, repeating video clip – the scene in my office, Dad in the straitjacket, me screaming at Mum, Stewart's silence in the car. I hadn't stopped being angry for a second.

Now that I'd started to get my real feelings out, I didn't know how to stop. When Stewart made me call my mum to find out what was going on, I knew I had to tell her about everything. Now that all this had happened, maybe she'd see things for what they truly were for once and actually leave my dad for good. The cycle had to end.

I called my aunt's house and Jocelyn answered the phone. She told me that Father had been released from police custody and immediately sectioned. Now he was in the same local psychiatric institution he'd been in after his other suicide attempts, and would not be released until he was "better". I listened in silence knowing full well that he'd fool the psychiatrist and be out within a day or so. I asked Jocelyn to fetch Mum.

By the time she got to the phone I couldn't hold back any longer – it was like an eruption of all the anger I'd swallowed back for so long, and she needed to know just what a monster Dad really was. She'd known we got beaten – that was one thing. She'd known we got verbally abused too. But there was something else.

That was when I told her what Sarina said Dad had done to her all those years ago. I told her that I'd known all about it and had to live with that fear. I was crying with rage, asking her how the hell she could have left us alone with him every damn night when she went to work, how she could have kept us all trapped in that house with him. We could have been safe. We could have been spared all that abuse. I really took it out on her.

Mum was spluttering and denying everything. She said she hadn't known anything about it. I knew she was lying, I wasn't going to take that, "What about the time when we were staying with Nan and Granddad because Dad beat Jocelyn so hard? We saw Sarina in town. She was a mess. That was when she and Dad were left at the house alone together. You knew how scared she was. You KNEW! – You must have figured something was wrong!"

I knew Stewart was sitting behind me with his head in his hands, hearing all this for the first time, but there was no going back. My feelings for my mother were finally set in stone. Not even when she was confronted with the truth could she admit she had to leave my father, or at least stand up to him and defend Charmaine, Jacob and Jocelyn. I couldn't take her denial anymore and so changed the subject.

"What's happening with the house?" I asked

"We haven't paid the mortgage for months and we've had a notice of eviction; the bailiffs will be here any day."

"So what are you going to do? Are you going to go to the Citizen's Advice Bureau to get some legal advice?"

"I dunno. I just dunno", she said blankly.

"Look, Mum." I tried a different tack, "If you divorce him you'll be much better off. Jocelyn and I will support you financially, plus you and the others will get some sort of benefits to help you. You'll get accommodation too. It'll all be ok. You won't have to deal with him any more."

Couldn't she see that our family could cope just fine without my father? Something good could come out of this horrible situation if only she just tried. I was sure she must have realised this deep down.

There was no response from the other end of the phone.

"I am going to go and visit your father at the hospital and talk to him."

"What? I don't believe it! Did you hear what I told you? About what he did to Sarina? After everything he's done to you, to his own children, all of us, for years?

You're still going to go and sit down and talk to that wanker and get his side of the story?"

"I love him Sam. I can't help it. I can't just turn those feelings off. Anyway, you must be lying. He didn't do that, he wouldn't have, he couldn't have. I would have known. I would have *KNOWN* about it."

"You *couldn't* have known! I was the one who protected them when you weren't there. I was the one who sat up till 1am every morning making sure I was the last of us to go to bed so I could be sure he never laid a finger on the others. I did it for years. I used to lie in bed waiting for the door to creak open and see him standing there. You had *no* idea what went on in your own house with your own husband and *children*."

There was a click and a burr noise. Mum had put the phone down on me. That was the last time I spoke to her.

I can honestly say that since that day I haven't missed her, or wondered how she is. To me, she is no longer my mother. She couldn't leave him for her own sake, let alone her kids'. To me she lived in denial. She'd rather block out the things her children tried to tell her than face up to the truth. She must have been scared that he really would kill himself and it would be on her conscience forever, but that same conscience could happily put up with seeing her kids battered and throttled before her eyes. One possibility that went through my mind was that maybe he'd worn down her self-esteem so badly she thought she'd be '*a nothing*' without him. Who knows. I just knew at that point that that had to be the end of it — I was through trying to speak sense to her, support her, comfort her and take the blame for everything that went wrong.

I dialled Sarina's number. I rightly assumed that no-one had bothered to let her know what had happened to her father. When she picked up the phone I told her to sit down and she knew straightaway that something was very wrong. I briefed her on everything that had happened the day before and told her where he supposedly was now and where Mum and the others were staying. She didn't really react, just listened.

Then I had to break it to her that I had told Mum about the things Sarina had told me so long ago, and she started to cry. I felt awful and tried to reassure her not to worry. I tried to encourage her that we would get through it all ok. I said I'd call her if I had any more news, but she said she needed to go to talk to Mum herself. I told her to take care of herself, and we both rang off.

A few days later Jocelyn called me at Stewart's and said that Sarina had gone round to the house when they were all there packing up their stuff before the bailiffs could come and take it all away. Sarina had confronted Mum, and Mum had broken down in front of her, apologising for what had happened while also claiming she'd never known what was going on. Jocelyn told me Mum was now panicking about whether any of her own kids had been abused too.

She'd grilled Jocelyn, who'd said nothing ever happened to her. Charmaine hadn't said anything at all since Dad had been taken away and Mum couldn't get a thing out of her. "Did he ever lay a finger on you, Sam?" my sister asked me.

I sidestepped the question and asked her what was going to happen next. "I dunno. I think Mum's going to visit him and see what he says and go from there."

I didn't like to think what Dad would tell Mum to persuade her to take him back, or just how quickly she'd give in. Since then I've had nothing to do with my parents and siblings and only occasionally visited my grandparents, usually at Christmas with a bottle of something as a gesture – I've cut myself right off from the rest of my immediate family. I understand the council eventually put them up in a bed and breakfast after that, and that Mum went back to Dad when he came out of hospital. In those first few days all my muddled thoughts and anger were combined with a massive sense of relief. I'd carried that burden of knowledge around for years, and now that it was out in the open I was grateful, even if Mum just took that as a cue to bury her head further into the sand and ignore what was going on at least it was off my back and someone else's problem now.

I just went into survival mode and looked after myself alone because I couldn't afford to help them any more. I'd done my bit, and they'd made their choice. You might find it odd, but they had never really seemed like "Family" to me. We'd been pitched against each other for so long that there was no love left. I knew that if I was going to stand a chance in life, I needed to be totally separate from them once and for all.

I went back to work later that week and everyone was tactful, giving me lots of support and never questioning me too much about what had gone on. I thought things might work out ok, but the situation changed overnight. I was still staying at Stewart's and one night he sat me down and told me he didn't think I was the same person he'd fallen in love with.

He went on to say he didn't understand what had happened with my family, and he couldn't really cope with it because it had changed his whole perception of me. He was right. Whatever I'd thought, I was no longer the way I'd been when I'd been desperately trying to cover up what was going on and show him a happy face. I was in shock, frustrated, and bitterly resentful, consumed with a whole host of emotions. I was giving him a hard time while he was being there for me.

He'd had enough. I begged him not to break up with me now but it was no use and he asked me to give him his keys back. The next day I walked into the office with my two carrier bags full of clothes, dropped them on the floor and burst into tears. I was homeless and alone.

CHAPTER 17

Talking it through

That night I went home with Faith, one of the sales reps at work. She knew what had happened to me and just took me under her wing without a second thought. She lived with a friend and assured me it would be alright for me to stay with her till I was back on my feet.

The next few weeks are a bit of a blur in my memory. I was still reeling from what had happened with Dad, Mum and Sarina, and shattered at the end of my relationship with Stewart. So much of my life – my past and the future I'd looked forward to with him – was blown apart and I had no idea what would become of me. I took sick leave from work. I didn't eat anything and stopped sleeping because I was plagued by nightmares and would wake up covered in sweat. I hit a crying jag that wouldn't stop.

Faith was sympathetic but insisted I go back to my GP, who diagnosed depression once more, and gave me a new prescription for anti-depressants. Again, she tried to persuade me to see a counsellor, but I still refused. I trudged back to Faith's with my pills and found her flatmate Alan in the living room. He was every inch as kind as Faith, and a really easy going, laidback person. He'd travelled round the world and seen a lot in his life. He took one look at me and sat me down with a cup of tea, asking me to tell him what was going on.

We sat and talked for three whole days and nights. It was amazing. We only got up from the bean bags on the floor to get a cup of tea or empty an ashtray. I can honestly say that I hadn't told anyone the whole story up till that point. It all came tumbling out − my parents, Stewart, my job, my past, my future. Everything. I felt that for once in my life someone knew the worst about me but still cared enough to listen. Alan just gave me his full attention. He wanted to know how I thought and how I felt; he asked me questions from time to time, or just let me cry and hugged me. Alan didn't want anything from me, and he didn't judge me once.

He did tell me what he thought, or what he thought he might have done in my place sometimes, but all that advice was for me to take or leave. He left everything up to me. One thing I knew I wanted to do if I ever got well was to travel like he had, and have new memories and experiences to shape me instead of my traumatic past, but just then I couldn't imagine ever recovering.

A few days after our big talk, Stewart came round to visit. Alan insisted on being there to make sure he couldn't upset me, and I was happy to have him there. He knew I was still in love with Stewart and was worried that I'd agree to anything he said or wanted if he'd only have me back. When Alan and I had talked I'd realised that I needed to be single, even though I didn't want to be, so that I could work out who I was and what I wanted from life for myself without the influence of a partner.

Stewart sat on one side of the room on the sofa and I sat in a chair opposite. Alan sat between us on the floor cushions, like a buffer. I could tell Alan's presence made Stewart uncomfortable, but I could also see that despite that he was genuinely pleased to see me. He made a little polite conversation about the weather and what was happening at work. After about an hour he left and when I walked him to the door he leant over and kissed me on the cheek. I remember wanting him to hug me and tell me that he'd be there for me and everything would be ok, but he didn't.

I closed the door behind him and walked back to Alan. Then I just threw myself on the floor and cried. Alan put his arm round me, cradled me and told me it'd get better in time. He gave me a tissue and I blew my nose and tried to explain how my family had always influenced my relationships with boyfriends. They hadn't liked Stewart because of the age gap, and I believed his parents hadn't liked me for the same reason, but we'd been so good as a couple and I loved him so much. I couldn't understand why he had pushed me away when I needed him most.

Alan was very down to earth about it. He told me Stewart couldn't possibly understand what life had been like for me when I was growing up, or the pressures I'd been under. His upbringing had been completely different – very privileged – my home life was the sort of thing his family read about in the newspapers and tut-tutted over. Alan was right, and I'd never seen it from that perspective before. It made more sense of Stewart's reaction, but it did make me wonder if there would ever be anyone who'd appreciate why I acted the way I did, without me always having to explain myself.

"Do you know what?" Alan asked me.

"What?"

"You haven't been outside this house for two weeks. I think you need a bit of a change of scene. You've got ten minutes to wash your face and put on something nice and then we're having a night out, alright? I think you need to see a bit of the good things that life's got to offer. Get your arse in gear, girl!"

I tried to say no because I just wanted to crawl into my bed and stay there, but he wasn't going to listen. He knew I'd never been clubbing or got drunk and had a good time. I made him promise never to leave me alone for one minute and he said he guaranteed he'd be by my side the whole night. While I went to get changed he ordered a taxi so we could hit London in style.

We walked through the West End surrounded by a swarm of people all joking, shouting and singing. I'd only ever seen the place on TV documentaries and Dad had made it sound like it was full of muggers and rapists but here I was and everyone was so happy. I couldn't quite take it all in.

Alan marched me into a pub that was crammed to the gills and bought me a Diamond White. We drank up and headed to a club where he'd arranged to meet up with his friends. We had a brilliant evening. I didn't dance – I didn't dare, but it was so busy that that didn't matter. I drank a lot more Diamond White and puked my guts up in the ladies loo but I had a lot of fun too. The bustle and the atmosphere was dazzling after weeks in Faith's flat and I found myself laughing along with all Alan's friends for hours.

When we got a taxi to go home in the early hours of the morning the driver drove us round and round in circles thinking we wouldn't notice and he could bump up the fare, but Alan spotted what he was up to. He told him to pull up by an alleyway round the corner from the flat and we stumbled out. Alan and the cabbie had a short argument about the fare and Alan said he only had fifty quid on him, so the driver would have to take that instead of sixty-five.

The driver didn't like that one bit and climbed out of the cab towards Alan, who grabbed me, flung me over his shoulder and ran off down the alley with the cabbie still shouting at him to come back!

Alan bundled me into a hedge and fell in after me and we sat there giggling, pissed off our heads and trying not to wet ourselves – we were both dying for the loo! The cabbie drove up and down the cul-de-sac for five minutes but never saw us and left with his fifty quid. Still hysterical, Alan and I climbed out of the hedge and pegged it down the road to the house. It was the first good laugh I'd had in a long, long time and something I would have never dreamed of doing while living at home. You haven't lived if you haven't run from a cabbie!

A couple of days later Stewart phoned, and it was wonderful to hear his voice again. He wanted to know if he could take me out for a drink and a chat; I felt strong enough and said yes even though I was unsure of his intentions. He picked me up from the flat and took me to the pub where we'd had our first date. I think he knew how much I treasured the memory of that first date.

It was nothing like our tense conversation of a few days ago, but almost like old times. We went back to his flat for coffee afterwards and the obvious happened. I didn't regret it for a moment. I loved him and wanted to be with him and was just so happy that he felt the same way. Over the next few weeks we continued to see each other pretty casually, or at least, we tried to be casual about it.

We hadn't really talked about everything that had gone on and I'd been so desperate to be back with him that I tried to let that slide, only there was an underlying tension. I was still very depressed and confused – if he'd dumped me on that day then he could do it again. He seemed to be trying to pretend nothing had happened.

A part of me knew that it couldn't last but I refused to admit that to myself. I needed someone there who I could rely on to care about me, so I kept on trying to piece things back together. It wasn't easy. The medication

I was taking was having even worse side effects this time round. I'd faint suddenly, or have blinding headaches that turned into horrendous migraines. I had a twenty-four hour blood pressure monitor fitted and my GP put me on beta blockers and watched me carefully. When the fainting didn't stop she signed me off work and sent me to a neurologist for a scan.

Obviously, it didn't help to think that as well as being depressed I might have something seriously wrong with my brain. In the end, there was nothing wrong on the scan, so I decided it must be the anti-depressants that were causing all the problems. I stopped taking them and was hit by another bout of withdrawal panic attacks. Eventually I stopped having the black outs and my hands stopped shaking, but that left me without any medication for the depression at all. I wasn't solving anything.

I did find myself a new place to live though. Faith and Alan had been great but the flat was so small I felt I was overstaying my welcome and I needed somewhere where I had a room of my own. I saw an advert in a local shop window for a lodger in a house nearby and took down the number. That's how I found Sheila and Gavin, an Irish couple who'd moved to England about thirteen years before then, and had two kids, a boy and a girl. I phoned up and went round to be interviewed by them and to my relief they seemed to really take to me.

I moved in in April 1998 and had my own room and a bathroom too – the first time in my life I'd had so much space to myself. No more sharing a room with my sisters or having my father rattling at the bathroom door. I'd never had so much privacy. I didn't have much by way of personal possessions to put in my room – just Alby – but it was a start.

Sheila was very polite to me, but she was also very insistent on knowing a bit about my family and how I'd ended up there. I suppose it looked a bit suspicious that I didn't have any parents coming round to visit. I can see now that she just wanted to find out what kind of a person I was and protect her family, but at the time I thought the best thing to do was to lie. If she knew my dad had just been arrested and thrown in a mental hospital I was convinced she would have chucked me out! The fact is, 'normal' people are scared about things they do not know, have not experienced and therefore do not understand.

I made up a story about my parents getting divorced and me moving out because I didn't want to get caught up in the middle of things. She accepted this, but one day when I came home from work she was waiting for me, and she really hit the roof. She'd bumped into someone who'd wasted no time in warning her to "be careful" of me because she was "mad" to let me live in her house. She'd demanded to know why, and this person had suddenly buttoned up and refused to tell her, so now she wanted answers from me.

She was so furious that she woke up Gavin, who came downstairs to see what was going on. I begged them both to sit down and try to let me explain. I warned them that they might be shocked, but I couldn't see any other way out. They had to know the truth too. The whole story came out and by the time I'd finished Gavin looked astonished. Sheila was weeping. She took my hand and apologised, while I just tried to say that the last thing I wanted to do was lie to them, but I'd been scared about their reaction.

After that everything was fine, and I lived with Sheila and Gavin for the next two years. Sheila once told me that they'd only meant to have a lodger for six months but they liked me so much that they let me stay as long as I wanted. It was the best possible thing I could have done at that time. I still think to this day that someone must have been looking out for me – finally!

I found myself in a new kind of world – a happy, contented family environment where everything was normal and nice. It was the home I'd dreamed of as a child, and I learned so much from just being there. They talked easily together and made plans for outings. They made wonderful meals and invited me to join them. I saw how Sheila and Gavin looked after their children and nurtured them, teaching them right from wrong. They took the time and effort to explain to them why a certain thing was done and why they shouldn't act a particular way. They asked questions and the kids could ask anything they wanted, and be sure of an answer. I soon began asking for advice from them and respecting their judgement. What the children said counted for something. It was completely unlike my own upbringing.

I could have ended up in a dodgy dive somewhere and met the wrong people, got involved with drugs and one night stands. Instead I was in the heart of a real family, with the perfect role models. Sheila and Gavin kept an eye on me too and I found that I could turn to them for advice and support if I needed it. Sheila was like a big sister, and really went out of her way to make me feel accepted. When I turned nineteen she threw me my first real birthday party and I was overwhelmed by her generosity and thoughtfulness.

Not long after I moved in I was walking home from work when a little red Corgi Gas van tooted its horn and pulled up beside me. It was Geoff, my old next-door neighbour. He was really pleased to see me and asked how I was getting on. He hadn't had any news since Dad's suicide attempt, and must have known that the bailiffs had taken most of our things. I explained that I was living with Sheila and Gavin and pointed out the house. He asked if there was anything I needed that he and his wife Mandy could get for me. I had to admit that I'd left home with only those two carrier bags, so if they had anything spare I'd be very grateful. He just said, "Leave it with me", made his goodbyes and headed off in the van.

That night there was a knock at the door. Sheila answered it and called me down from my room, saying I had a visitor. There was Geoff standing in the hall. I was a bit surprised but thrilled too. I introduced him to Sheila and Gavin and he joined us all for a cup of tea and some small talk. Then he beckoned me out to his van and wrestled a TV out the back of it, telling me to grab some bags that were in there too.

We lugged everything up to my room and Geoff put down the telly on the dressing table and rubbed his back a bit. He told me that he and Mandy thought these things would help me on my way. I opened one of the bags and found a brand new dressing gown, a kettle, an iron, some towels and some other bits and bobs they'd had spare. It was wonderful and I didn't know how to begin to thank him.

Geoff just fussed around plugging in the TV and then he pulled a card out of his black leather jacket pocket, "This is from all of us. Don't read it till I've gone though." Then he smiled and said, "Sam, we always knew you were the different one in that family, and we always thought you'd get out of it somehow. We only know some of what you went through but we just want you to know that if there is ever anything we can do for you, you know where we are."

This was almost too much. I gave him a big hug and fought back the tears. Why would anyone be so kind to me? What had I ever done for them? It took me years to understand that they didn't want anything from me at all; they were just sincere, friendly, honest people and they cared what happened to me. At the time, standing in my new room surrounded by their presents I just felt unworthy of it all.

After Geoff had gone I opened the card. Thirty pounds fell out, and I read the note:

Dear Sam,
Just a little something to help you on your way in your new home. We are here for you if you ever need us.
Love Mandy and Geoff
PS buy yourself some food, and don't go spending the money on fags!

I did as I was told and spent the cash on groceries, and I kept the card too. I still have it. A week or so later I went round to see Mandy, taking her some flowers to say thank you for doing so much for me. I hadn't got to know her very well at my old house, but after we'd had a coffee and a long, long chat together our relationship blossomed from there.

Not only did I have Gavin and Sheila, but also Mandy and Geoff, to bolster me through a truly terrible time. I had no family and no boyfriend and years of curfews and those bullies at school meant I didn't have a very big network of friends either. Mandy and Geoff were always there for me, and if anything they adopted me into their own family. It was their house I went to at Christmas, when they'd spoil me rotten.

If Mandy went shopping she would make a point of buying me a top or a treat of some kind and bring it round for me. She tried to teach me how to be gracious and accept a gift without feeling overwhelmed and getting upset or suspicious. "Just a simple thank you is enough", she'd tell me when I got flustered and started saying I couldn't accept things.

If they knew I was home alone they'd ring up and invite me over for dinner and keep me there chatting all evening. They understood that I craved a normal kind of life, and someone to rely on. Their generosity could be breathtaking.

That first year when I was free from my parents I managed to take and pass my driving licence. I wanted to buy a car, but it turned out I wasn't as free of my parents as I'd thought. Their bad credit rating meant that the bank wouldn't give me a loan and I had to go through all sorts of procedures to prove my financial independence. Eventually they were persuaded and I bought my Nova.

I was really pleased with it but a short time later it broke down, and I didn't have any spare cash to have it fixed. Mandy and Geoff insisted on lending me the money, telling me I could pay it back whenever I could afford it. I wanted to pay them back bit by bit, but Mandy said it would be fine to pay it all back in one go when I could afford it. I saved for months, but when I tried to give the money back to Mandy she wouldn't take it, "You've shown me I can trust you, and I loved being able to help. Don't worry about paying it back, spend it on something else!" I'd never been given such an extraordinary gift, and it was totally unexpected and gratefully appreciated.

I could sit down with Mandy and talk to her for hours about anything and everything. I really bared my soul to her and Geoff, and I could do that because they had never once judged me and I knew they would never hurt me. It was more than that sense of security I'd known when I had a boyfriend. I would have done anything for them, and they for me.

Mandy could be quite strict with me too. If I did something she thought was wrong she'd let me know about it, no beating around the bush! She gave me another perspective to think about. After a while I began to learn to think things through before I rushed in impulsively, or made the wrong assumption, and that was all down to Mandy's influence. The two of them cleaned up my bad language too. Everyone in my family swore pretty much all the time and thought nothing of effing and blinding instead of expressing what they thought in more subtle terms and of course, this had its effects on me! They set up a swear box, but it wasn't the money that stopped me swearing, but the knowledge that it upset Mandy and Geoff and wasn't a good way to behave, really. Not the kind of lesson I'd learned when I was a child.

That time with Mandy and Geoff was the closest I ever came to feeling complete. But I've never got rid of the same loneliness I've always carried around with me. Wherever I went, whoever I met, people always talked about their family and that was really hard to cope with. Obviously I couldn't explain my own situation every time someone asked after my family, so I found myself constantly hiding and putting on a new façade.

I was always trying to please everyone else, and though sometimes that could be a good thing, very often it meant I ended up doing something I didn't want to. I felt guilty too because I thought that if someone like Mandy, Geoff, Sheila or Gavin made a kind gesture it meant that I owed them. My self-esteem was still so low that I could take the tiniest thing as an attack, and it would strike me to the core.

After my weird, isolated childhood with its messed up rules and topsy-turvy morals I found myself struggling with everyday things in my new life. The same low self-esteem that made me think I wasn't worthy of Mandy and Geoff's love also made me think that other people were judging me or getting annoyed with me, when in fact it just wasn't the case. Because I didn't know how to act I would end up rubbing people up the wrong way, then getting defensive when they got exasperated with me. This just made me even more self-conscious.

I'd turn to Mandy for advice and she'd reassure me that there wasn't necessarily a good or bad way to do everything. She tried to explain that lots of people go around finding fault with others because they think they know better, but actually nobody's got the right. The way Mandy saw it was that you shouldn't judge someone unless you can say you know exactly what they've been through in life. And how many people can do that?

I think at the time it was almost too much for me to take on board, but the things Mandy told me were backed up when I had therapy later. The message was simple. I didn't have to justify myself to anyone, so long as I was true to myself and what I believed in. The thing was, back then I couldn't begin to work out what it was that I *did* want and believe.

CHAPTER 18

The "chatterbox"

I lived every hour of the day with what I called my "chatterbox". This was a kind of monologue of thoughts that ran through my mind constantly, and undermined me over and over again. If someone looked at me strangely, the chatterbox would say they disliked me, or knew something about me. If I did something well at work and my boss praised me for it, the chatterbox said she didn't mean it and was only humouring me. If someone wanted to be my friend the chatterbox said it couldn't be true – who'd want me as a mate?

The chatterbox told me I was nasty, spiteful, uncaring and a liar. I didn't exactly "hear" it as my parents' voices, because it wasn't a hallucination – it was my own thoughts – but the message was the one Mum and Dad had drummed into me my whole life. I wasn't worth a damn.

The technical term for the influence a parent has over their children as they grow up is "preconditioning". Even if you think, like I did, that you are rebelling against it, your character is formed by what they do. My sisters and brother and I had been preconditioned to be confused, angry and resentful, thinking that the world was against us. And ultimately it made us secretive and defensive.

These were all in themselves symptoms of the depression that I was now slowly beginning to understand I had suffered from my entire life. I had never had any outside interests because my parents wouldn't let us have hobbies, so there wasn't much apart from boyfriends to distract me from my moods. I didn't have the energy most of the time anyway. I would cry for no reason at all; I thought it came out of the blue, but it was just sheer, constant unhappiness.

I've often wondered if I would never have got ill if my parents had been "normal". I'll never know that for sure, but if things had been different I'm sure my parents would have noticed that I was heading into a decline and tried to do something about it. No such luck.

I first started to look for some answers when I was living with Gavin and Sheila. The cycle had to begin somewhere. Something or someone must have turned my father into the tyrant he was. He'd once told me that he'd been abused by his own father and mother. Sarina had hinted that she'd heard stories too, which made me take it more seriously than a lot of his tall tales. I had only met my grandfather a handful of times and I knew he'd split up with my grandmother and remarried. As well as that terrible time Dad flung my Christmas present back at him, I had also made several visits to see him with Sarina. He used to like to measure our heights with a mark on his shop wall every time we came, so we could see how much we'd grown.

I saw a local newspaper article about my grandfather, saying that he was selling his shop in town after many years and moving on. In it he said, "he was sad to go, because he'd made a lot of friends over the years". It didn't sound like anyone from our family! I decided to seize the chance to go see him again before he left. He might be the key to unravelling the whole mystery behind my father's behaviour.

It took guts to go and ask him some hard questions though. When I walked into the shop he didn't recognise me at first, but when I told him who I was he leaned over the counter to give me a kiss. He looked so much like my own father that I felt totally unnerved. The shop hadn't changed much, in fact I could still see the scribbles on the wall that showed me at age eight, nine, ten …

Nervously I kept to the point, just trying to get the questions out. I think I told him straightaway that I was having nothing to do with my parents any more since Dad's suicide attempt, and that I needed to know a few things about Dad's childhood. I asked if he had beaten my father, and he denied it. He obviously hadn't been expecting this kind of inquisition, and became very grave. I hesitated and then made myself ask if it was true that my grandmother had somehow abused my father the way he had claimed. My grandfather looked shocked and said angrily, "No, of course not. Your grandmother is in hospital now. She's very ill. If you're so keen to ask that kind of question you can go and ask it to her face."

I backed out of the shop without saying anything else. I'd never met my grandmother. I couldn't show up on her death bed and demand to know if she was a child abuser. After that day I just let go of the idea of finding out where all the cruelty had begun. If there was any truth in what my father had told me, my chance of confirming it died a short time later with my grandmother. And what if she denied it too? How would I know who was lying?

I actually don't think there would have been an answer that would have satisfied me, because I don't believe that even enduring horrendous abuse yourself is any excuse to act it out in turn on a defenceless child. At some point you have to take responsibility for your own behaviour and break free from the pattern of violence and negativity. I was struggling to fight my own way out of the cycle, but I barely knew where to start. Whenever I thought I was getting somewhere, my background dragged me back down again.

I was still in love with Stewart so I wanted to take things slowly when I started dating a new boyfriend. This new guy was a great person, reliable, honest and attentive to me. We went out with each other for a couple of years and did very well together considering that my depression was not improving. I kept on avoiding counselling, and was still trying different prescription drugs, hoping to find something that would "cure" me once and for all. I went to work, saw my friends and had good times with my boyfriend, but my whole life was undercut with nagging doubts and the chatterbox, which kept up the same demoralising message that I was a bad, worthless person.

The worst thing about this relationship was that my boyfriend's mother decided she didn't like me, and set out to spoil things. I'd been honest about my family when I met her, but too blunt for my own good. I was still working out how to behave with people and what to tell them so I just flat out told her that my dad was insane, my mum was not much better and that I'd walked out on them after years of terrible treatment. She didn't like that one bit! It was the same scenario as with Stewart – that sort of story was something she read about in the papers, not something she could possibly ever begin to understand.

She did try to be kind on occasion, but eventually she didn't always bother to make much of an effort with me even if her son was there. I think she thought I wasn't good enough for him. She'd call him when we were trying to spend some time together and send him off on errands, leaving me on my own. I was sleeping more and more heavily as the depression weighed in on me, and if we were staying at her house she'd complain that I was treating the place like a hotel if I didn't get up promptly. That was something I found increasingly hard to do; I was physically exhausted the whole time.

I honestly didn't know how to handle the situation at the time and probably didn't ease the situation much by taking things out on my boyfriend, who was torn between the two of us. I'd rant at him, trying to push him into proving he cared more about me. He'd try to be diplomatic. God knows what his mum was saying about me behind my back! Mandy took my side and tried to give me advice when I went round to cry on her shoulder over something his mother had said, but it was no good.

In a mixture of courage and anger I abruptly told my boyfriend that we couldn't see each other any more because I was damned if I was going to get so much hassle from somebody else's family after all I'd been through with my own. He was really upset and tried to tell me he'd talk to her again and things would be different, but I knew this was the only solution. He later confided that he'd told his mum he could never forgive her for the way she'd treated me; that was cold comfort for me. At least I knew there really had been a problem and it wasn't just that I was being too touchy and sensitive.

I was only twenty-one and at this age I should have been having the time of my life, but instead I seemed to be spiralling further and further downwards. The chatterbox was as vocal as ever, and after this latest split it made everything spin out of control, and I all but lost the people closest to me. Mandy and Geoff had really liked my now ex-boyfriend, and a few months after we'd parted ways I found out that they were still seeing him socially.

I was terrified that they must all have been talking about me, and of course, according to the chatterbox, surely that would end up with them all hating me? What if they told him more things about my background than I'd ever wanted him to know? I'd opened up to Mandy and Geoff and suddenly I felt exposed. My emotions were all over the place because I also saw it as a betrayal. If Mandy and Geoff really loved me, why did they stay friends with him after all his mum had done?

I went rushing at Mandy, demanding answers, and understandably she was exasperated with me. It wasn't as if they'd done anything to make me doubt their love. They just liked my ex, and that wouldn't affect the way they saw me, and they promised they wouldn't give away my secrets either. I did listen, and on one level I did understand, but my old defences were still in place. I was back to seeing everything in black and white and I couldn't get my head round it. I wanted everything or nothing, and that's how I let paranoia ruin my perfect friendship with Mandy and Geoff.

They did their best to reassure me, but I think they also thought I was being too jealous and possessive of them. I had clung to them and I thought that nobody, not even Sheila and Gavin, would ever understand me as well or treat me so kindly but I still backed away from them after that. I thought things could never be the same. You could call it cutting off your nose to spite your face, but that's the kind of logic paranoia gives you – I love these people, and that means they can hurt me, so I'll be safer if I keep away from them.

It couldn't have happened at a worse time. I'd changed jobs a few months previously because I didn't like the fact that everyone in the old office knew about my family history – paranoia again. I loved my new post, which was a step up in the world, and my boss and workmates were great. I went out with them all quite often, and there was a relaxed, friendly atmosphere. Shortly after I'd started to distance myself from Geoff and Mandy, though, the company went bust and I found myself out of a job. This brought a whole new train of fears for me. I didn't want to sign on because I thought it'd mean I was just sponging off the state and was no better than my parents. I was also taunted by the panic when we were little and the bailiffs came round while we were all dragged to hide behind the curtains in the living room, barely daring to breathe.

I plunged straight into anxiety without even trying to do anything practical. Luckily a friend from my old workplace, Matt, stepped in at that point and took me firmly in hand. First he took me to the dole office to make sure I'd have an income, and see that I started to apply for new posts. "It's not the end of the world, Sam, there's loads of jobs out there, and you have the ability to do anything you want to", he comforted me.

Then he made another suggestion. He knew I'd always wanted a dog, and he overrode my protests that I couldn't get one now with hardly any money coming in. Mandy and Geoff had always been against me having one too. Matt wasn't bothered, and marched me to an animal rescue home and we spent hours going from kennel to kennel. Matt didn't exactly have his work cut out for him – I was desperate to have something of my own to care for that would love me unconditionally too. It was obvious I wasn't going home alone!

In the end I fell for a lovely mongrel bitch who was only a few years old, and I called her Boe. She played a massive part in my life from then on; you could say she became my family. She'd had a rough start in life too, and however ill I got I always had to be sure that Boe was fed and walked. She got me out of bed in the morning and was there to greet me with her tail wagging when I came back from work in the evening. I think we both depended on each other.

CHAPTER 19

Trying to hold it together

Matt was right about work. It only took me a week
or two to find a new job with an international finance
company. I had to drive further than I was used to to get
there every morning, but it was a huge company and the
salary was better than anything I could have dreamed of.
I started a new relationship there too, almost straight
away. There was a guy at the desk next to mine called
Dan who didn't talk to me for two whole days when I
first got there. I thought he must be an arrogant idiot, or
just plain unfriendly.

After a while I couldn't take him sitting there ignoring
me any more and asked him flat out in an attempt to break
the ice, "Are you usually this rude or do you just fancy
me?" And he smiled and blushed at the same time – the
ice was broken. We started dating and I was back in my
old, familiar romantic whirl. He was smart and sexy and
everything was exciting and passionate. I was "up" again
and felt stronger with him to cheer me up and make me
feel great about myself.

He introduced me to a whole new way of living
where we were constantly on the go. He had a big circle

of friends and we were always going out for dinner or to the pub. Every weekend there was something different to do, like going to a football match or some crazy kind of extreme sport. Dan was really adventurous and I liked to indulge him. I bought him a bungee jump and loved the expression on his face when he thanked me, full of exhilaration and excitement. That was so successful that I treated him to a paragliding lesson and he liked that so much he considered taking it up as a hobby.

I didn't want to join in because I was much too scared, so I found myself on the sidelines watching him have the time of his life. I thought that was enough. His parents were very good to me too, and happily adopted me into the family. I found myself round at their house for dinner a lot, always greeted with kisses and smiles. They liked to know how I was and what I was up to, and didn't seem to care about my background. I was much more careful this time about what I told them, but though they must have known something was wrong, they never held it against me. They couldn't have been more accepting of who I was, how I spoke, what I did, said thought and believed, and I became a fixture at their family weddings and parties. I think I needed them as much as I needed Dan himself.

The trouble was, this time round it wasn't enough to keep my depression at bay for long, and I found myself pressuring Dan and testing him. If he said he loved me, I had to demand proof. I couldn't take anyone at their word if they were being nice about me. The chatterbox kicked in, and I alternated between outbursts of emotion and clamming up to try and protect myself. Of course, in reality I didn't need to protect myself from Dan, but from my own inner voice, but even though I was beginning to recognise a pattern in my behaviour I couldn't stop myself and only saw what I was doing after the event.

I ignored the warning signs for months. At work I couldn't concentrate on anything for any length of time. When I got home every evening I'd climb into bed fully clothed and snooze from six till eight thirty when Dan came in from the gym, then I'd talk to him for a few hours before climbing back into my bed and falling into a sleep that felt like a coma. If I was asleep, I didn't have to think about what was going on, and that state of soothing peacefulness was how I imagined death would be – a haven from all my panics and struggles.

I regularly slept through my alarm and by midday work was torture because I just wanted to go to bed. I couldn't stay interested in anything for long, so in the end I just started to doze away all my spare time. I could sleep from a Friday evening through to Monday morning, waking only occasionally.

I either comfort ate, cramming in food that I could no longer taste, or forgot to feed myself. I was getting through packets of cigarettes at three times my normal rate. On the occasions when I did go out with Dan it was really hard work. I found chatting about the smallest things draining and after an hour I'd pretend I had a headache and go home. I didn't think I was energetic enough to keep anyone entertained, so I didn't bother to keep in touch with friends.

I couldn't even watch the telly or read a paper. The news was always bleak and made me feel like there really was no point in living in this horrible world. A drama like *Holby City* would play on my mind because I couldn't cope with someone dying or people being affectionate to each other. If I saw an NSPCC advert I was wild with contradictory feelings. I couldn't stand the fact that children suffered that way, but I was also resentful because nobody had come to help me when I was at the mercy of my family.

My one effort to get better consisted of buying some marijuana and smoking spliffs from time to time, hoping it would lift my mood. If it did, it didn't last very long. In the morning I'd wake up groggy on top of my usual depressed sluggishness. I was seeing less and less of Mandy and Geoff by this stage and had moved into my own flat, which made it easier for me to sink into gloom.

All my old insecurities were back with a vengeance. There was nothing that Dan and I didn't row about. I didn't like some of his friends, and didn't always want to go out with them because I thought they were saying things about me, or else I was just too tired. If he argued back, I'd argue harder. If he shouted, I'd shout louder. When we went out I felt like I was just going along with something I didn't really want. It began to dawn on me that I was doing things for him but had no idea what I wanted to make myself happy.

I had been badgering my doctor for months, insisting that the medication was not working any more. She found another antidepressant for me, Efexor, and for the umpteenth time she told me that I really should have counselling. I was so worn down and confused that I couldn't be bothered to argue it anymore and just agreed, even though I honestly believed that what I had gone through at the hands of my parents wasn't anywhere near bad enough to justify it. What would I have to talk about?

I suppose that might seem bizarre, but I couldn't keep one thought in my head for long enough to give it any kind of consideration. My doctor explained, "The Efexor should keep you on an even keel while you're doing the counselling – I'll keep an eye on you and adjust the dose in case you start to feel worse. The counsellor's name is Stephanie, and she works in the surgery. You know this place well, so I'm sure you'll feel safe with her. You start next week."

I was stunned to think I was finally going to have to talk to a professional counsellor like this and didn't know what to expect. It would involve dragging up all that stuff I'd been trying to bury, and having to tell someone all the embarrassing details of – oh God! – the bucket full of piss, having the lump in my breast, my father and Sarina … How was that going to "fix" me? I might be Stephanie's first lost cause, or she might think I was a whinging cow who'd been a burden to everyone around her and that in fact I was fine.

I phoned Dan and he listened as I poured out my fears, then sighed and said, "Sam, it's the right thing to do. I'm amazed you've agreed to do it, but it's bound to be good for you. I'm," he paused, "really proud of you. Do you want me to come with you the first time?" That was typical Dan. Despite all I'd done to him he was completely understanding and ready to support me – whatever it took to make me feel better.

I hesitated because the prospect of going on my own was unnerving, and if he was there to hold my hand I could probably face anything, but I had a sudden clear realisation that I had to do this alone. I needed to be honest, and strip away all those things I was hiding behind if I was going to find out who I really was. I thanked Dan from the bottom of the heart, but said I'd do it on my own.

Next week there I was in an unfamiliar room in the surgery, sitting opposite a quiet, polite lady who hadn't asked me a single question. She just sat there calmly, watching me, and waiting for me to say something. The room was very plain with no pictures on the bare cream walls. There was a small table with a tray of pebbles and a box of tissues at the ready on it and a skylight instead of windows. There were no distractions.

The room was silent, but my head was buzzing with anxiety. My throat seemed to have seized up and my lips might as well have been stitched together for all I was able to open them and begin. Where was I supposed to start? Did she think I was crazy already or would that bit come later?

I thought about giving her a sort of a cast list to introduce her to the members of my family and somehow quickly say why I didn't see them any more. Very controlled, very easy. Just a few facts rather than my opinions. Then if she said something back I'd have a foothold and I could work out how to handle the rest of the conversation. I just couldn't imagine what the hell she was thinking about me and that bothered me.

I was irritated, "I don't know where to start." She put her head on one side and looked encouraging. "There are a million and one things going through my head. I don't know where to start." I was beginning to sound angry.

Then she finally spoke, "Tell me a little about you."

It broke the tension, and all my half-articulated thoughts came spilling out, as if they were falling over each other in the rush.

"My parents … they've attacked me, abused me … they *taunted* me. I hate them, I think I have to hate them. Everything they ever said to me just grates. I don't want to think I'm their flesh and blood. I just think … I keep thinking to myself one day they will vanish, one day they'll die … one day I won't have to worry about them being there any more and I'll be ok, I'll be free … but I'm stuck till then, I'm really trapped. It's claustrophobic. I'm not them. I'm not a part of them, I have *never* been a part of them but I thought I'd be better when I left home and I'm not and I'm really, really scared that I never will be."

From that point on, Stephanie delicately steered me through weeks, then months of counselling. I would bring up some incident and she'd ask me a question about it – just getting me to explain who a certain person was or something simple like that. That would lead me to another incident, and more questions, and another memory. As we went on I realised I could trust Stephanie totally. I would cry over certain things and she'd just hand me a tissue and let me get it out of my system. Then I'd dry my eyes, nervously fiddle with the tissue and carry on.

She used to tell me that I should be proud of myself and that I was lucky to be able to do all this at such a young age. A lot of people go through their whole lives without looking at the things that are holding them back, or they come to them so late that it's harder to work through their issues and change their habits.

At the time this gave me some comfort because it made it sound like one day I would be probably be ok. I began to trust her and feel safe to tell her anything. It was odd because although she was endlessly encouraging, she also kept her distance and remained professional, sitting self-composedly on the same chair on the other side of the little room.

Bit by bit, a lot of my childhood came out. Some of the stuff I talked about I'd never told anyone – not Alan or Mandy or any of my boyfriends – but there were still things I didn't dare tell her because they were too shameful. I would break off halfway through a story and say something was my fault. Stephanie would just turn the question back to me and say, "Why was it your fault?" I'd stammer out something like, "Because I should have stopped it happening" or "Because I shouldn't have said that."

Without giving away what she thought herself, she'd just say, "Well, what else could you have done?" Sometimes that brought me up short because I realised that I couldn't have done it differently. When I faltered she'd encourage me to say that out loud, "There was nothing else I could have done." That was a revelation.

When I began to have difficulty remembering things or just getting the whole story out coherently she suggested that it might be easier if I wrote things down between sessions. I kept notes then, and it really helped. It gave me something to do if I woke up with a bad memory because I knew that it was safely recorded in my notepad and we would be able to talk about it next time we met.

When I was angry with my parents and swore I'd never forgive them Stephanie would say in a maddening way that of course I'd be able to understand them in the end. I'd argue back that I had lost my childhood forever, and one day she told me a wonderful thing – that when I had children of my own I would be able to experience a childhood I had never had through my children. That thought has stayed with me ever since and I believe in it utterly. It became one of my sparks of hope to look forward to, in that far off time when I was going to be "well".

Mostly it was slow progress. My new antidepressants were better but my doctor still had to up my dose after a few months. To be honest, the counselling left me even more mixed up and dangerous to myself and others. Now that the Pandora's Box was open I was losing control. My random crying became worse because now even my defensive façade had gone and I was completely raw and vulnerable.

I would turn minor incidents into major eruptions and made life hell for those closest to me. I had always been scared that counselling would have this effect, and now my worst fears seemed to be being acted out. I didn't know what memories would come back to me at each session and I couldn't guess how I'd react. I'd suppressed some of them so heavily that I'd pushed them right out of my mind, and now I relived them so vividly that they left me shaken, angry and completely confused all over again.

I knew now that I was capable of committing suicide and I was haunted once again by the idea that I really would breakdown this time and lose what little self-control I had left. I was petrified I would end up howling and straitjacketed. The image of my dad being pushed into the ambulance replayed itself in my mind.

The thing was, I just didn't know what to do with all this knowledge and these emotions. Nothing made sense, and as I found myself hitting out in all directions I worried that I had really lost the plot. What was I looking for in all this pain? I couldn't explain how I felt to anyone near me. I knew I was overreacting but I couldn't stop myself. I felt more and more isolated.

CHAPTER 20

An unbearable loss

I still visited Mandy and Geoff but things were still strained between us because of my paranoia: I suspected that they weren't making the effort to get to know my new partner, Dan, and concluded that they didn't want me in their lives any more. I wasn't exactly lovable when I was going through counselling, either.

One night the phone rang and I answered and was surprised to hear Mandy's voice; she didn't sound like Mandy. Her voice was tight and she seemed to be crying. I felt a jolt of fear.

"Are you OK, Mandy?"

"Not really, Sam." She took a deep breath. "I'm phoning to tell you about Geoff. I thought you had the right to be one of the first to know." She appeared to be struggling to compose herself.

"Go on."

"There is no easy way to tell you this, Sam, but Geoff has cancer."

I felt as though someone had my heart in a vice.

"Sam, are you there? Everything is going to be ok.

He has to go for some chemotherapy and have some medication, but the doctors think they can help."

"I'm still here, Mandy. I don't know what to say." And I burst into tears too.

"Come over and see use, we can have a chat together."

I put the phone down and found I couldn't stand up. This was a nightmare; I even pinched myself to test that I wasn't dreaming, but I was all too awake. Boe came over to me, blinking with concern. She always knew when there was something wrong. She licked at the tears on my face and then lay down in front of me submissively, paws in the air. I leant over to stroke her and cried on and on. This was the worst news I'd ever received in my life. Geoff was so kind, funny and just so *good* that I didn't see why he should be dealt this card. My father deserved cancer, not Geoff.

I tried to wipe my eyes then threw on a coat and some trainers and drove over to their house. All that night we sat huddled together talking about Geoff's condition and what the doctors might or might not be able to do to save him. We swore blind that there were cures for this now – surely he would be fine? I was committed to believing he would because the alternative was unthinkable. It was cancer of the lymph nodes, caused by smoking.

The next few months were hell. I was caught between a need to see Geoff and the fact that I was convinced that I had no right to spend precious moments with him. I thought that honour belonged to his family and I mustn't go to them to talk about my problems any more because they had enough to think about. Mandy would call me and give me updates on his progress, only it was obvious that he wasn't getting any better.

He was offered antidepressants but refused them, and was being dosed with morphine to take the edge off the pain. He was losing weight fast and was no longer the cuddly Worzel Gummidge I remembered as a teenager. I had been on the edge of a breakdown when he was diagnosed, and now I tried to preserve my memories of him as he had been. I had to tell him some very important things before he left us, though, because I couldn't bear for him to be gone and me to be tormented with regret for not talking to him.

I was still in my shaky relationship with Dan and we were planning to go on holiday that June, but Mandy was anxious that Geoff wouldn't be alive when we came back, so she invited me round to see him before I went away. Dan came with me. Poor Geoff could hardly speak but he still had that glimmer in his eye, the glimmer of love and warmth that I will never forget. It broke my heart to see him so ill. He whispered, "How's the counselling going?" and I told him what I honestly believed – that I wanted to get better and I was sure I would one day. "It's hard though, and it's really knocking it out of me."

Then Geoff did something that brought me to tears and that will stay with me for the rest of my life. He made me promise that I wouldn't give up, "Make me proud of you, Sam, I want you to be happy," he murmured. I swore

I would, wiping my eyes and sniffing. He looked at Dan and whispered, "And you look after her." Dan nodded and promised he would do his best. He must have been really tired and it was clear that we'd have to go and let him rest. I couldn't say goodbye because I knew it would be the last time I saw him, but he just gave me a wink and gave me in an embracing goodbye cuddle, rubbing my back and then Dan and I quietly left the living room.

Mandy was waiting in the kitchen to see us out and I gave her a card for Geoff that I'd written the night before and couldn't face giving to him myself. "Ask him to read it when I've gone," I said, and Mandy smiled bravely and said she'd make sure he did. The card read:

"You have been more of a father to me over the past ten years than my own. I have been supported, accepted, guided and loved by you and for me to put into words exactly what you mean to me would be impossible. I know that if I didn't have you and your family in my life I would never have gotten as far as I have and I owe so much of my progress to you. I will never forget you. I will always love you and no-one will ever be able to take your place. You have made such a positive impression on me and you have given me reason to believe that there are people in the world who do care and do want to see me get somewhere. My gratitude to you for all the love you have given me will never be forgotten ... I love you."

The next day I came home from work and found a message on the answerphone from Mandy, "Sam, I'm just calling to say that I gave the card to Geoff and he was really moved. It meant so much to him, Sam, he cried. It was a lovely thing of you to do."

Dan and I went away to Spain and came back; a few weeks passed. Each time the phone rang I shuddered in case it was '*the call*' from Mandy telling me Geoff had finally lost his struggle. He was still holding on, but getting weaker by the day.

One particularly grey morning I woke up with a feeling of foreboding. I went about my usual routine of showering and getting dressed and headed into work, a sense of unease creeping in. Nothing felt right. Work passed slowly, and at one point I looked up to see my manager Louise looking at me in a concerned way and asking if I felt ok. I told her I didn't really, but couldn't quite put my finger on why.

Louise wasn't just my boss but also a close friend and confidante and she knew what I was going through. She'd always been there to chat or give me a hug when things were really bad. She told me to take care and went back into her office, still frowning, and I decided on the spur of the moment to make an appointment after work to talk to my GP. I was seeing Stephanie for a counselling session too, but I still went ahead and booked my appointment with the doctor.

Usually I wouldn't run to her just because I was having a low day, but something inside me felt very strange and different. Louise let me leave work early and I made my way to the surgery. The receptionist knew me and said hello, though she seemed a little more reserved than usual which I put down to her being busy or having other things on her mind.

I took as seat in the waiting room and a short time later my doctor poked her head round her door and winked at me. I smiled and she stood back and beckoned me into her consulting room. We sat down.

"How are you, Samantha?"

"I'm not sure. I don't really know."

"Do you want to tell me what's happened?" she asked gently.

"Oh, nothing out of the norm!" I said, trying to make a joke out of it.

Her tone changed, "You haven't heard, have you?"

"Sorry?"

The look on her face told me everything.

"Samantha, it's Geoff."

This time it was my tone which changed – I almost screamed at her, "What? What's happened?"

She shook her head and looked at the surgery carpet.

"Has he died? Tell me!" I had lost it now and was shouting, not even at her, but because I was frantic with fear.

"I am so sorry. Yes, he passed away very peacefully in his sleep, early this morning."

My body tensed up and I began shaking my head, clenching my fists. The pain I experienced was physical, wracking me through. I started to wail – there's no better word for it – like I was barely human,

"No, no, no. It can't be. He hasn't died. This is a nightmare, it's not *real*. It's not *real*. Tell me it's not true!" I clutched at my doctor desperately and she tried to cuddle me. The room filled up with people; the receptionist had heard the commotion and raced in to see what was wrong and the two other GPs were standing in the open doorway staring at their feet. My doctor explained what was going on. Stephanie appeared at my side, and began to stroke my head, pulling my hair out of the way as I sobbed madly.

They handed me some tissues and told me that I could cry as long as I wanted to and get it all out of my system. A second wave of realisation hit me and I thought about never seeing Geoff's gentle face again or being able to talk to him and I started to breathe too fast and hyperventilate. The receptionist disappeared and reappeared with a brown paper bag and the doctor held it to my mouth and told me to take deep, slow breaths.

It took me half an hour before I was stable enough to even get up from my seat, and then I went upstairs with Stephanie to talk things through. I don't like to think what would have happened if I was on my own when I found out. I am convinced that Geoff played a part in making sure that I was in the safest place I could have possibly been in. Everyone was very calm and very professional – they just moved in and looked after me.

This time Stephanie pulled her chair up to mine and fetched a fresh box of tissues. I was hot and sweaty and the crying had left my face purpled. I had a steady, pounding headache and my chest felt tight. She cupped my hands in hers and pulled them into her lap as I shook violently.

"Sam, we can sit here and talk as long as you like. Take your time."

I have to pay tribute to Stephanie because she had endless patience. My fear gave way to anger, and I went between weeping and shouting, demanding to know why Geoff had had to die. There were no answers to the questions I asked, and Stephanie just nodded or shook her head and let me ride out the storm of emotions. I must have been there for an hour or more before I had recovered enough to get myself home safely. Even then, I don't remember the drive at all. All I could think about was Geoff and how his family were grieving and in pain.

CHAPTER 21

Losing control

Geoff's death was the beginning of my last, rapid slide into clinical depression. At that point I fell into a kind of trance. I was oblivious to everything – Dan, work, friends. Louise gave me a week's compassionate leave which I was grateful for, but I wasn't much better when I returned, and when she tried to talk to me or give me sympathy I felt a million miles away.

I had withdrawn myself from life completely. I still went to counselling but I had dried up. I couldn't think of anything else to talk about and I was stuck. I just thought about Geoff 24/7. Everything else was a haze. The funeral was extremely hard. I wanted to speak and Mandy had agreed that I should but I only got a few lines into my speech when I burst into tears. Mandy and the children looked on, smiling encouragement through their own sorrow and tears, and somehow I made it to the end. I had thought the funeral might bring me some closure if I could talk about all Geoff meant to me, but it didn't work that way and I missed him more than ever.

If ever I had a heartfelt ambition, one I cherished even above having a home and kids, it was to make Geoff proud of me. I had to try harder to get what he wanted for me. It was the only way I could possibly attempt to repay him for all his love and generosity.

Whenever I got so low that I was contemplating suicide the promise I'd made to him would echo out of the depths of my mind. It was as though it was branded on my conscience. I would argue with it, exclaim that it was too hard. I was bone-tired with fighting it. I couldn't remember the last time I had any energy. I couldn't carry on. Then I would think of Geoff and picture his face if I told him I was giving up. He would have been so disappointed in me, and however ill I got I knew I couldn't let him down and break that promise.

There would be a twinge of guilt and then a flash of hope somewhere in me and I knew Geoff was giving me the courage I needed to face another day. If I needed an answer to a question I would catch myself wondering what Geoff would say, and letting him guide me. Every time I made a decision I "asked" him what was best, and took comfort in knowing he was still with me.

For six months after his death, he was all I could focus on. The fact that I couldn't *get* happy was putting a strain on me and Dan. I wasn't totally honest with Dan about my feelings and then got furious with him when he couldn't see that I was bored or upset. Instead of just telling him he had done something to upset me I'd throw a child's tantrum.

I couldn't stop to think what damage I was doing to him or to me. We were growing apart but I was determined that that wouldn't happen. Mandy was dealing with her own grief and trying to support her children as they mourned their father. I felt guilty because I thought I couldn't help them, and that pushed me further away from them. If I turned to Louise again I was scared she might suggest I couldn't do my job any more, then I'd be broke and back on social security and ... My thoughts spiralled off. I didn't want to give up Dan or his friends or family when I needed them most, because I thought I'd only have Boe left. I was trapped again. Every harsh word I flung at Dan concealed a terrible fear of loneliness, and I struck out blindly.

I was haunted by awful thoughts of harming myself. I imagined myself holding a knife to my throat or slicing my wrists slowly, watching the blood pour out. I saw myself climbing on the dining room table in my flat and hanging a noose from the light fitting. I'd put my neck in the rope and step off the table. I could picture my throat swelling and the rope burning my neck, my mouth frothing and my body fighting for life one more time before going limp. These played out in my head every day, and I was only free of them when I slept.

I'd always been meticulous about how I looked because I wanted to be as different to my slobby parents as possible. It was a point of pride with me to have freshly washed hair, once or even twice a day. My nails would be painted neatly with a whitener painted on the underside to make them immaculate. My make up was done with precision and I wouldn't even step out of the house without eyeliner.

Now things began to slide, and I let my nail varnish chip away in flakes. I couldn't be bothered with washing my hair and just screwed it up into a pony tail. Then I cut all my locks off to within an inch of my head. My counsellor Stephanie told me that she thought it was retaliation against my father, myself and the world and could be a sign of a re-birth for me. I dismissed it as 'crap' and said I'd just fancied a change and couldn't be bothered to keep making the effort with it, but looking back now I can see that it was exactly that! In time I stopped wearing my make up too, and that's when a few people commented on the change in my appearance.

Eventually it all came to a head and what happened next was catastrophic. One night in the heat of an argument with Dan he told me he had had enough and was ending our relationship for ever. There would be no more kissing and making up – heaven knows our truces had got briefer and briefer. I couldn't stand it. There was nothing I could think of left to say that would stop him, so without thinking I grabbed the biggest kitchen knife I could find and edged towards him as he was hastily packing his things, threatening to put it to his throat.

"PLEASE don't leave me!"

Dan must have been terrified, but he called my bluff and I knew I couldn't do it so I put the knife to my own wrist instead, "Then I'll kill myself!"

It had finally happened. I had turned into my father.

Dan begged me not to pull that trick, "I am going though, Sam. I have to. Don't be so stupid." I think he believed I wouldn't really do it, and I dropped the knife and just pleaded with him not to go, but he took his stuff and, white-faced, disappeared into the night.

When the door had slammed behind him I broke. Every nasty, untruthful thing I'd hurled at him came back to me in a flood. I'd aimed to hurt him, so he couldn't hurt me, but I hadn't meant any of it. He hadn't done anything to deserve it. I collapsed on the floor in hysterics. Boe had been cowering under my bed in the next room because she was sensitive to all the shouting, and now she crept out and solemnly came over to me with her tail between her legs, ears flat against her head.

I reached out to her and she sat down beside me on the carpet. I began to stroke her slowly while my mind raced. She was all I had. I had no family. I was so low I'd started to cut out my friends. Even if I'd told them what I'd been going through and they'd been sympathetic, I wouldn't have believed a word they said. I had been low before, but now I went into freefall.

I had tried so hard to be normal and happy. I'd done everything I'd believed I was supposed to do, after all. I'd held down a good job and had a lovely boyfriend. I stayed solvent and I'd once had a full social life, and I'd still been miserable. What the hell was wrong with me? All that was left of the life I'd been trying to build was crumbling before my eyes; none of it was doing any good. It was as if I was back were I'd started from, alone and crying. All I did was hurt people.

My life had become a collage of negative thoughts – not good enough, not happy enough, not nice enough – and I spent my whole time trying to piece them together and understand what was going on. It was a constant search for the pot of gold which I'd believed as a child was at the end of the rainbow, and I had gone nowhere.

The chatterbox was whispering a new message to me now, enticing me, encouraging me to take action. It said that if I killed myself everyone would be better off without me. I'd be free too, and out of the cycle of highs and bitter disappointments that had made me so bone tired and weary I could hardly wake up in the mornings. The chatterbox said that my past was a lie and my future would only get worse, and now there I was, pulling knives like my father, threatening the people I should have loved most. Better to be out of my misery. Better to be dead.

I pressed the knife firmly against my wrist, building up the courage to slash the thick blue vein that was pulsing under my thin skin. Boe started to bark and I looked up at her, startled. Her brown eyes were frantic, and she licked me again, then barked, beside herself.

I began to wonder who would look after her if I was gone. Who was going to love her as much as I did? What if she stopped eating if I wasn't there? She'd have to go back to the rescue home. I couldn't leave her.

I steeled myself and tried to think clearly. The only person I could think of to call was Stephanie. She answered the phone and talked to me as I mumbled and wept, never once getting impatient with me even though the call went on for hours. She told me to come into the surgery first thing the next day, and I promised I would. She also said I could ring her again if I was scared, no matter what the time was.

Somehow I made it through the night, clinging to Boe as if she was my last hope. Yes, I was overrun by thoughts so dark I could barely face them, but somewhere even deeper than that there was a spark that wouldn't be extinguished. I wanted to live after all that I'd had to take, and I couldn't give up yet, whatever the chatterbox told me.

I went straight to my doctor in the morning, in sheer shock and disbelief at my behaviour the night before. I had petrified myself this time, and I owed it to Geoff to save me from myself. I had come so far and could not give in now. I crawled into her office looking like a wreck because I hadn't even had the strength to wash my face. I hadn't bothered to phone work and call in sick, but I just didn't care. My eyes were so swollen from crying that I could hardly see anything.

I couldn't look her in the face. Straightaway she came over to me and put an arm round my shoulders. She handed me a tissue from the ever-full box on her desk and said, "It'll be ok, Samantha, everything will be ok."

Shakily and incoherently I stuttered, "I thought it would be better after the funeral …" but Geoff's funeral had been months ago. "I don't think I can cope. I talked to Stephanie last night … I think … I think I wouldn't be here if she hadn't answered. I had a knife … I nearly did it."

My doctor let the whole story come out. Then she said, "Look Samantha, I think you need a break. I think you need some time off. You've been seeing Stephanie now for a year and I think we need a change of tack. I'd like to refer you to a hospital for a while."

CHAPTER 22

Safe at last

"Hospital" was a word which scared me. To me in this instance it meant straitjackets and padded cells, doctors pumping me full of medication and locking the door shut behind them as they left. It was the last resort, wasn't it? I knew that if you were sectioned you couldn't leave of your own accord, and now that I'd found out that my dad had been hospitalised several times, I didn't exactly have much faith that it would cure me. It didn't seem to have done anything for him. Perhaps I was incurable too.

I sat straighter in my chair and faced up to my GP, "I am not being put away. I can't go to hospital, I've got a job, and I've got Boe to look after and my rent to pay. It's not possible. I can't just take a holiday!" My doctor held up her hands and told me to calm down, "You've got good medical cover and you can stay in an excellent private hospital. It'll be voluntary, and you can just go for a few weeks if you want to."

"But ... Don't you doctors use that line on everyone? Just to get them to go quietly?"

She smiled, "Have I ever lied to you before? I haven't given you any reason to mistrust me. Will you wait a minute while I make a phone call and see if they have a room available?" She dialled while I sat there with a host of thoughts running through my mind, listening. I heard her say, "Oh, that's such a shame. She was a lovely girl – how are her family coping?"

I realised with shock that she was referring to another patient who had obviously committed suicide. She must have been just like me. That was the most decisive turning point of my life, because I didn't want that scene to play out again, to have my doctor saying "she was a lovely girl" about me too. This was my last chance to save myself from being a statistic.

She put the phone down and told me there was indeed a room for me, and I could go there for dinner that very evening and see what I thought about it all. "You won't have to stay if you don't want to, no-one's going to force you."

I stayed silent. I had to go, but still …

"Samantha, if I let you leave here now and don't send you to at least have a look at the hospital, I'm worried that I'll never see you again. Can you honestly tell me I have nothing to worry about?"

I shook my head, "You're right … I'll do it. There's nothing left to try."

After I left the surgery I drove home to Boe, who greeted me ecstatically, jumping up and down. I reached for the phone to tell Dan what had happened and to ask him if he'd stay in my flat and look after her while I was away. He responded well and told me he'd do anything to help, and did I want him to drive me to the hospital that evening? He said he'd explain things to Louise, who would make sure no-one else at work knew. "Everything will be taken care of Sam, don't you worry, you are doing the right thing."

Minutes after I rang off he was at my door. When I opened it he stepped straight in and put his arms around me. I could barely believe it after all the horrible, wounding things I'd said only the night before when I'd been so far gone that I'd threatened him with a knife and here he was, holding me close and promising me it would all be ok. Dan was nothing short of amazing.

I put a few things into an overnight bag in case I decided to stay and we got into Dan's car and drove all the way to the hospital without saying a word. It was a typical wet and dingy February evening and when we pulled up in front of the Cardinal Clinic in Windsor it looked more like a hotel or a stately home. I stayed in the car, unable to move. I fished a lighter out of my handbag, rolled down the window and lit a cigarette.

"I'm really proud of you for doing this, Samantha," Dan broke the silence, "Are you OK?"

I stared out of the open window and exhaled a stream of smoke, "Yep, fine! I'm just about to check into a lunatic asylum, I've split up with my boyfriend. I've probably lost my job and no-one will ever want to know me after this. But apart from that, I'm fine."

Dan didn't bother rising to my sarcasm and simply put his hand on my leg and said sympathetically, "Just take your time. I'll come in with you and I'll be looking after Boe. Stop thinking about everyone else. You'll be fine. You'll get better."

I climbed reluctantly out of the car and shut the door hard. I turned to face the entrance and took a deep breath before marching into the hospital, Dan trailing uncomfortably behind me, unsure of what to expect.

The people at reception knew who I was immediately which un-nerved me because I wondered who had said what about me to them. I remember wearing a jacket buttoned up past my neck and a cap covering my face as much as possible – I felt ashamed, I wanted to hide, I didn't want people to know who I was and why I was there. We were asked to take a seat in the waiting area, which doubled as the music room. I watched people who looked perfectly normal walking by, chatting and laughing. A lady came over and introduced herself as a psychiatrist, "shall we go and have a chat in private? Your friend can come too if you like." I knew that if Dan came too I wouldn't be able to talk freely to the woman, so I asked him if he wouldn't mind staying behind. Dan nodded nervously, unsure of his surroundings, and I followed the psychiatrist to a little room. I worried about what Dan was making of the place.

The psychiatrist was pleasant, but distant. She asked me a few questions about myself – my feelings, my history, a little about my family. She wanted me to tell her what had happened in the last twenty-four hours, and I was completely honest. I didn't see any point in hiding anything from her – not the knife, or the fact that I'd smoked marijuana, even though I was paranoid that I might be arrested for it! While I talked she made a few notes and nodded. "I think it'd be a good idea if you stayed here for a few weeks. What do you think about that?"

Throughout the discussion I hid my face behind my cap and didn't look the psychiatrist in the eye until I asked, "If I want to go, I can, can't I? Any time?"

She smiled, "Of course. No-one will make you stay, and no-one will make you do anything that you don't want to do, but I'd recommend you stay here for at least two or three weeks." She led me back to Dan so I could break the news to him that I had decided to stay. A nurse soon appeared and told me her name was Penny, "I'll show you round the place and take you to your room." I must have looked alarmed; I still didn't really trust what was happening. It all seemed so unreal. Dan came with us on a brief tour of the hospital, which seemed clean and bright, not the sort of loony bin I'd had in mind. But I will admit that I was waiting to be shown the straitjacket room at any moment!

I had a small room with a single bed and an en-suite bathroom. There was a television, a phone and some drawers for my clothes. Penny said I could personalise it if I liked and put up some pictures, "It's yours. You can make it your own. Whatever makes you feel more comfortable."

Dan stayed for dinner although neither of us ate and then he sat with me for a few hours, but eventually he gently told me that he had to get going because Boe had been on her own all day and would be bursting for a pee and wanting her dinner, "I'll be back to see you tomorrow, and I'll text too and call you. Alright?" I walked him to the door but it was hard to say goodbye and turn back to my bare room now that I was alone among strangers. I lay down on the bed.

I could see nothing ahead of me. There was no reason why I should continue with my life. All I had ever experienced was pain, as far as I could tell, and I couldn't live with that eating away at me any more. It was like a black hole, and I wanted to crawl into it and never come out again. I wanted to be cocooned there and never see the light of day again. That way I'd never feel anything again, and I could be safe. I thought the black hole was winning, and that any part of me that had once been truly alive was now being crushed.

What else would free me? That blackness had become a part of me; how else could I deal with the rage it made me feel, or the nightmares it sent me? I was letting it swallow my pride, my motivation, my dignity and finally my life. Here I was in a mental hospital, who knew if I'd get out? What were they going to do for me here?

Would they tell me why a person doesn't love you, or why my relationships always went wrong? Why everyone who was good in my life had either died or left me? Or why my past kept coming back to beat me down again? Could they teach me to be happy? I just wanted to be normal and to look forward to things. I wanted to have energy and strength, and not crumple up in a ball at the slightest setback.

I was there because I had tried everything else, but I doubted this was the solution, but it had to be my last chance before I took that step from which no-one comes back. Lying there in the narrow bed I didn't know if I was safe at last or just on the brink of a last descent. I didn't think I could take any more.

There was a knock on the door, and Penny came in. She had brought me a glass of water and a tablet. No-one had said anything about tablets. I panicked, "What's that? The doctor didn't mention pills. Why do you want to give me that?"

"You don't have to take it if you don't want to. It's just a sleeping tablet in case you feel worried about being here the first night. I know it's hard being somewhere different and new like this."

I knew I'd struggle to fall asleep so I reluctantly decided to take the pill. Penny said good night and I pulled up the covers and dropped off into a deep sleep.

CHAPTER 23

The big pink bubble

The next morning there was a knock and Penny came in with a cup of warm coffee, "Do you want breakfast? You can have it in your room this morning, but after that you've got to come and join us all at the breakfast table." I didn't normally eat breakfast – a legacy of those childhood mornings, locked in my bedroom with my sisters – so I refused, but she said she'd go and get me some grapefruit anyway. "It's really important to have a healthy breakfast."

I sat in bed with my coffee, pushing the grapefruit segments round the bowl for a while. Then I opened the welcome pack that had been placed by my bedside table. A sheaf of papers fell out, full of lists of activities I could do during my stay: anger management, yoga, music, art ... It wasn't at all what I'd expected.

I made it through my first day in a state of high anxiety, but I tried hard. Everyone, staff and fellow patients, was very friendly. The place was more like a nice hotel than a lock-up. There was something liberating about the fact that there was no point in keeping secrets. If someone asked me a question about why I was there,

I could be totally frank, after all, they knew I was there because I was very sick and suicidal and so were they. I found myself making friends.

On the outside they looked every bit as normal as me, but I could see that they were suffering from the same depression and confusion as me. For a fellow sufferer it was clear as day – the way I'd catch them staring out of the window into nothingness, or playing with their hair aimlessly. I knew that – I did that. I could see them trying to put on fake smiles too, and I recognised myself.

I had a programme to follow which kept me busy, so busy that I was exhausted. It seemed odd, because I thought I was there to think about myself and instead I was bombarded with information. I did creative writing, flower arranging, yoga, aromatherapy, physiotherapy, reflexology ... There was something called "contact class" which was all about teaching us to connect to one another, either physically or by mentally acknowledging someone.

One exercise we did was for the nurse or psychologist in charge to sit us all in a circle and throw a cushion to someone, who had to say their name and tell everyone something that made them happy. Then they had to throw it to the next person, who would give their name and come up with something that made them happy too, and so it would go on until everyone had had a chance. Then we'd sit and talk about the things that had come up.

I think everything I did made me think hard about an aspect of my life, or a cycle of thought I'd become trapped in. All the therapies worked in different ways. One of the major hurdles I faced was dealing with my anger. I was crammed with tension. I was angry that my father was still alive while Geoff had been taken from us, that my parents had got away with abusing me and my sisters and brother. I was angry that I was reduced to being in hospital.

Before I could begin to tackle my depression I had to remove the anger, which was obscuring that deeper feeling of sadness.

One thing they taught us was that "the only reason you are angry is because you are not getting what you want." That doesn't sound very profound, but if you think it through it makes sense. I couldn't undo what my father had done and have a perfect, innocent childhood. That just wasn't going to happen, however angry I got. Nor would Geoff come back, even if I wanted it desperately. By getting so furious I was just fixating on my past at the expense of moving forward.

Instead I had to take a deep breath, re-focus my thoughts and ask myself what the problem I was getting so worked up about really involved, and if it was a situation I could change for the better. If I couldn't change it, I had to let it go. If I could, I had to see what was holding me back, and what the worst thing that could happen might be. Usually, when I looked at it hard, it turned out not to be the end of the world.

I found other ways of dispersing my anger too. I could rip up newspapers, or thump a pillow, but one thing worked best for me. The clinic had a swimming pool and at one end was a hanging punch bag. I'd picture my father's face on the bag, his hands tied behind his back, and then I'd lay into it, punching and punching and punching till my fists were torn and my arms ached, my heart pounded so hard in my chest that I couldn't hit out any more. Releasing that physical charge of energy was amazing; it was my safety valve.

I was also taught how to relax. I don't think I'd ever really known how to do that, even if I'd thought I was managing it by sitting in front of the telly with a coffee, that was far from the case. It seems very strange to have to learn how to do something like that, but it was one of the hardest skills I had to learn, mainly because I had hardly ever been calm in my life – I walked on eggshells the whole time, waiting for the next outburst from my father. Depression is usually accompanied by anxiety – the two are so closely related that they are almost indistinguishable. The niggling effect of anxiety wears the sufferer down into depression, and the constant negativity of depression makes your thought processes turn in on themselves – anxiety.

Anxiety was what kept me confined to my home, in my "safe zone"; I wasn't relaxing when I sat there with the TV on and a mug in my hand, I was merely avoiding things that wound me up. If I wanted to go into town and buy something and couldn't get Dan to go with me, the trip would turn into a trial of nerves. I would worry that people were looking at me, and might recognise me and then I'd have to talk to them. I might not be dressed right and people might be laughing at my fashion sense. My family might appear from nowhere. What if I got to the counter and I didn't have enough money to pay? Or what if I got lost?

When I got anxious my palms, underarms and back would sweat. My hands would tremble and my chest would tighten with the beginning of hyperventilation. My throat would constrict, too. My breathing would affect my thinking because I wasn't getting enough oxygen and soon I'd be terrified. Sometimes all this happened before I'd even got out of the house, and I'd just stay put instead, wasting another day indoors, hating myself.

The most basic thing they introduced me to in hospital was deep breathing. At the first sign of uneasiness I had to concentrate on my breathing and draw air right in so it felt like it went all the way to the pit of my stomach. Then I had to release it slowly; it was no good doing it all in a rush, that would just lead to me gasping frantically and panicking more. If I did it right the worst would pass, and I could ask myself what it was I was so stressed about, and if it really was all that bad after all. I'd see solutions to all the fears: if I didn't have enough money, I could take something back; if someone wanted to look at me, so what?

That was for emergency situations, but the hospital also worked to give me tactics to use to stop myself even getting to that kind of pitch. Yoga sessions showed me a way to focus totally on my body and breathing. My chatterbox plagued me in the introductory class, telling me I looked stupid and that I was getting it all wrong, but in order to do the poses correctly I had to phase it out and concentrate on what my body was doing, and not what the chatterbox thought.

I had a massage a few times a week, too. Initially I felt very awkward allowing someone who wasn't a lover to touch my bare skin, but the massage therapist picked up on that and was very sympathetic. She tactfully began by giving me only reflexology, or foot massage. I fretted over why I was so self-conscious about my body; I knew about the scar from the time I'd fallen on the broken fish tank, but was there something else that someone had done to me that I'd now blocked out? Did I really think someone here would try and take advantage? I knew they wouldn't, but it still left the uneasy question of why I was so scared. I was troubled by memories of my dad jumping on me when I was in the corridor outside the bathroom.

After a while I felt more comfortable and she moved on to giving me whole body and head massages. She'd add lavender oil to the stuff she was using, and I found that soothing. One of the nurses suggested putting a few drops of it on my pillow when I went to bed, and I was amazed how well it worked. There was a physio who tried to do something about my painful shoulder, which felt locked with all the tension I'd carried around with me for so long, but I think she hardly had time to make a start on it in the time I was there.

I kept up the habit of having an occasional massage after I left the hospital and it made a great difference to my ability to handle stressful situations. When your normal state is anxiety, it's harder to recognise those first signs of a panic attack. With a calmer attitude, I could see when my attacks were kicking off and tackle them before they got out of control.

It wasn't the case that everything was simple. We had group classes in relaxation too, when we all lay round on mats and the teacher talked us through breathing exercises. The trouble was, some patients unwound so much that they fell asleep and started snoring, which wasn't exactly restful for everyone else. Once or twice I got up and left the class, but then I realised that that just meant that I was missing out, and letting myself get worked up to boot.

One day we were all stretched out on the floor and the first rasping snore started up. My temper began to soar and I sat bolt upright and demanded, "Who is that?" Everyone around me opened their eyes and stiffened visibly. "It's doing my bloody head in." The teacher had switched off the music and was just standing there, so I apologised and said why I had a problem with it. "What do you think we should do?" she asked.

I got decisive, "There's only one thing", and with that I walked over to the snorer, grabbed the end of his mat and dragged him towards the door. People started to laugh and someone jumped up to help me tug the offender out into the corridor. Then we shut the door behind him and got on with relaxing. After that we didn't have any more problems with snorers.

One of the things we covered was called "creative visualisation" and it proved invaluable to me when I left hospital. If something annoyed me during the day I had to just let it go without dwelling on it so I could deal with it later, when I had the time and was in the right frame of mind. Brooding over and over again on something when you're in a passion only leads to getting worked up and blowing things out of all proportion.

This way, I'd wait till I was somewhere quiet where I could think quietly – when I'd left hospital, I usually used my bedroom for this. I'd get comfortable, and start to focus my thoughts. I would envisage myself in an isolated, safe place like a deserted beach where there would be no "interruptions". The sand would be white and soft beneath me and the clear, blue water would lap softly on the shore. I'd picture a big pink bubble floating above me.

The bubble could be as big as I needed it to be and would never burst. Nothing I put in it could get out again. I'd think of everything that had upset me during the day and put it in the bubble – a person, a harsh word, a wrong thought, anything. When the bubble was full and my mind was exhausted, I'd just blow at it and off it would drift across the sea and over the horizon. Doing the exercise made a great difference to me; I still do it now, nearly every day. It can take a while to do it properly without feeling stupid and letting other thoughts get in the way, but if you persist it works like a charm.

CHAPTER 24

Finding closure

On my third day at the hospital I got some cards in the post from a few friends who'd found out where I was. I had very mixed feelings about it. I couldn't help wondering why they hadn't noticed how bad things were before; I suppose they must have thought I was coping somehow. I went through agonies imagining conversations they might have about me with people who were less close and that made me apprehensive about leaving. Did they really care or were they just easing their consciences by dropping a card in the post?

I was cut off from the real world in hospital and who knows what it might have decided about me by the time I got out.

It seemed to be a pretty common fear. We had group counselling sessions where fifteen or twenty of us would sit in a circle, sharing our fears, or episodes from our lives. If the psychologist in charge didn't like the way things were flowing, they'd throw something else into the discussion and we'd all have to be honest about our reactions. The first time I said nothing, but I gradually began to join in because I understood that we all had to make the most out of our time there by being honest. That was the way to progress, and I didn't want to be in hospital for any longer than I needed to be.

The trouble was that the people who had been there longest tended to dominate the talk, and they only wanted to air their fears about leaving – how would their colleagues react? How could they explain what had happened in those few months away? This got very repetitive and didn't help everyone else who was at an earlier stage of therapy.

Eventually, some friends and I tried to break the pattern and launched some other topics into the ring. This *really* shook things up! Some patients couldn't cope at all. One screamed and ran out of the room. Plenty of others burst into tears. It was chaos! A far cry from our usual, demure therapeutic chats. I felt terrible, and afterwards I went to talk to my psychologist and tell her how guilty I felt. She was unphased, "Samantha, if they couldn't deal with that topic then that's their problem and it's something they've got to work through. I don't think you did anything wrong. Those sessions help different people in different ways – so don't worry about it so much."

The staff were always on hand to help, whether in or out of the official classes. They coaxed me out of my room and told me to mix a bit more with the other patients instead of holing myself up with a pile of self-help books, "You can read those when you've left here, but you should make the most of what's on offer now.

Besides, whenever you say anything in the group sessions it sounds like psychobabble you've got from those books!" Chastened, I saw what she meant. Putting my problems in language I'd borrowed from a self-help manual wasn't the same as getting to grips with them.

Once one of the nurses noted that my mood was failing and surprised me by saying, "It's only human to have good and bad days. That'll happen when you're well too. Stop fighting and just let it be." Given the situation that seemed an extraordinary thing to say. We were all meant to be trying our hardest to be happy, weren't we?

I see her point now, though; a bad day doesn't mean everything will come tumbling down. We've got to be able to withstand a bit of fluctuation because we can't be happy all the time like Stepford Wives. The ability to cope with up days and down days has to be built into the way we tackle life, or else we're just forcing the same reaction to everything we encounter. I try to keep that in mind now, and be philosophical about my day-to-day moods.

I had a few visitors too, but mostly they left me confused, although they meant well. Guests from the outside world meant that I had to build up my barriers again and behave differently, just as I was having to strip that kind of thing away in order to deal with my problems. I thought I might scare them off otherwise. I'm sure part of them was just curious to see what the hospital was like too, to reassure themselves that I wasn't in a straitjacket with bars on the window.

When you're lower than you've ever been, a simple touch, a cuddle or kind words can go a long way to helping you to heal. I took comfort in the smallest gestures people made in order to make it through to the next day. I missed Boe because she had always given the same kind of unquestioning affection. A couple of times in the evenings Dan brought her to see me but we had to sit in the car as the hospital didn't allow us to bring our pets in. I kept her picture by my bedside and hoped she didn't get too upset about me being away. She'd kept me alive on that terrible night when I almost turned the kitchen knife on myself.

Two people who did make a real difference were Dan's parents, Lesley and David. They had always made it clear that they didn't care about my background and just took me as they found me, and I bet they'll never really know in how many ways they helped me to recover. They were my second "true" family, after Mandy and Geoff, especially as Gavin and Sheila had separated by this point. I was under their wing from the first day I met them, and not even when I put their son through so much pain did they make me feel like they had given up loving me.

I've always found it hard to understand why anyone would like me, because that's the lesson that was drilled into me all through my childhood: I was worthless, nasty, selfish. Dan's parents gave me a reason to believe that not everyone is judgemental and hurtful. Just by being them, they made me put my trust into the, good experiences I had had with people in my life. There was a better way of living out there and they were proof.

In hospital they brought me daffodils and a pink writing pad so I could get my thoughts out on paper. They left me so happy that I desperately wrote how I felt on the first page of that pink pad – I couldn't bear the idea that I might forget it.

I used the pink pad for my creative writing classes too. The teacher asked us to write a letter to someone about a specific time in our lives and how we had felt then. Then we all had to read out what we'd done, and we talked about it. What I wrote was very special to me, but it went so deep that it took me a while to understand it. I didn't even give it a title till sometime later when I was in a group therapy session, and I knew it was called "Goodbye".

I had written a letter to Geoff.

'Goodbye'

Someone here at the Clinic told me that I may feel better if I wrote a goodbye letter to Geoff. Geoff passed away peacefully on 23rd July 2002, he had cancer and was a father figure to me. He had accepted me as one of his own children.

I felt protected, supported and loved; something that I never felt with my own parents. I have struggled to say goodbye because I suppose that I do not want to let go, I do not want to say goodbye, goodbye is too final when it comes to death.

I know I do not want to say goodbye, but I know as well that I will see him again one day. I take comfort in the thought that he is looking over me and guiding me through life. I am worried that if I say goodbye, I will be on my own again and I don't think I can cope with that loneliness

The pain of feeling alone is too much for me to accept or want to experience again and I'm scared of that.

Before Geoff died, he told me not to give up, he said that he knew that one day I would get to where I so desperately want to be, happy and contented with life, but that I mustn't give up along the way.

I could never really feel as though I could trust anyone; my own parents didn't care about me, they were cruel and abusive. How I managed ever to trust anyone is beyond me, but I instilled my trust in Geoff and I am hurt and scared that he isn't there for me any more.

No-one will ever be able to answer the question that burns so deeply in my soul: why Geoff was taken away from me and the people that loved him so much, and why someone like my father is still here.

I suppose if I thought long and hard, I did manage to trust someone once, I had managed to put my trust into one person. Maybe it is because I am so conscious of that that I am struggling to ever envisage trusting anyone ever again?

I just don't want to hurt anymore; I don't think I could cope with the pain. It is easier for me to remain defensive and unattached because at least that way, my feelings won't ever be hurt again if anything happens to another person that I love so dearly.

I believe that in order to have a solid base for moving on in my life, I need to be able to put some trust in some people maybe that is why I am stuck, because I am struggling to do that?

I don't want to be frustrated and angry at myself and others anymore, I need to move on with my life. Please someone, help me, I can't say goodbye.

CHAPTER 25

Finding the real me

In the weeks I was in hospital I was never really aware of making rapid progress. Recovering from depression, like falling into it in the first place, was a gradual process. If I had a dramatic breakthrough it was there in that letter, courtesy of Geoff – I had to move on. I had to resolve my past, which meant letting go of my anger, facing my fears, *trusting* people, accepting things that I could not change: Geoff's death, my ruined childhood. I hardly knew it at the time, but my stay in hospital gave me the basic tools to do just that.

The core of all this hard work was the one-on-one therapy sessions I had with a psychologist. It was a different experience to my meetings with Stephanie. Stephanie had encouraged me to bring things up and talk about them, get upset about them. My new psychologist made me challenge that emotion and look closely at the way I acted when I got upset. I had to break down my thoughts stage by stage and see how I'd got there: a small, everyday tiff with a boyfriend would gather momentum and make me angry and depressed because I had subconsciously linked it to something that my parents had done to me.

Or I let one setback make me believe that everything was wrong and I was powerless to make anything good of a situation.

Incredible as it may seem, this was the first time I understood how everything connected together. I wrote this book with the benefit of that hindsight, so when I've described events from my childhood I've also shown how they made me act in a particular way, but until my time in hospital I didn't see that link for what it was. I was just blindly battling my way through a tumult of memories and jagged feelings.

Once I understood what I'd been doing it was easier to unpick those connections too. I could go about my everyday life without the black hole opening up again and swallowing me.

It would take a long time, especially as my mind had been "trained" over the years to think that way, and I still wrestle with it on a daily basis, but now I think I can win. I'm human, things will upset me. Like the nurse said, I would have good and bad days. The important thing was that I monitored myself and kept in touch with my real feelings. Was I furious because someone was rude to me at work for no reason, or because I had taken years of verbal abuse from my parents and those bullies at school?

Just as Mandy had told me, no-one was better than me so I didn't have to answer to anyone but myself. As long as I didn't go out of my way to be spiteful to others, why should anyone criticise what I did? If that person was rude to me out of the blue, that was their problem, rather than *my fault*. And the over-the-top anger I was feeling wasn't aimed at the colleague at the photocopier, but at my father's behaviour.

It was a lot to take in, and the task of changing the way I thought was daunting. When my therapy began I left sessions condemning them as a waste of time. I didn't think talking could do me good anymore and looking back at them, they were very difficult for me. I had to talk about things I had never spoken about, not even to Stephanie, and take a long hard look at myself and my fear. When you can't see the solution in sight, that's a desperately hard thing to do.

I realised how much I'd let other peoples' opinions guide me and mould me, and just what a façade I had built to cope with not being "the real me". I'd had an inkling all those weekends when I stood on the sidelines or when I'd gone along with something that I didn't, deep down, want for myself, but this was the first time I really understood it. I'd pretended to be happy and confident, and I rarely let that mask slip, even when I was with the small number of people whom I trusted. Keeping up those false pretences was a full-time job and damned hard work at that and I had to admit that by denying my past I was running away from myself. It had a knock on effect too, because I resented people who liked the "fake" me, because I thought they weren't bothering to find out who I really was and how depressed I had become. The trouble was, they didn't have much chance of doing that, because my mask was so fixed that I had become a mystery even to myself. Now all that had collapsed, and I was left stripped bare.

I had made efforts to change my personality in the past, which was a co-dependant way to act. I tried particularly to match up to the idea of what I thought my boyfriends or their parents wanted, but I'd only added layers to the façade. When I tried the opposite, it ended up being something like, "If you don't like me, steer clear", which was aggressive and pushed people away. Simply put, it was black or white with no in-between.

I didn't like the personality I'd built, and now I had to start from scratch and work out what I really wanted for myself and just how I would live my life if I was honest with my feelings. Who was I and what did I want from life? I wanted the good things, but I just didn't know how to get them for myself. I was starting from a disadvantage with my history and the burden of depression, too.

I'd wanted to be free of it all, and now I could see just how much slow, excruciating effort that would involve. I drew up a mental checklist to follow that would help me re-train my mind from the harmful habits of a lifetime:

First: Realise that you are thinking something negative – maybe someone complimented you and you thought they couldn't mean what they said and were just buttering you up to get something else from you.

Second: Argue with yourself – is it really as negative a situation as you think? Have you misread what's going on? Are you overreacting? Why shouldn't they give you a compliment?

Third: Ask yourself where that negative thought actually came from. Perhaps *you* think you don't deserve that praise – that's why you think it's not genuine. It's got nothing to do with what the other person's motives might be.

Fourth: What do you really think about it? Accept that compliment for what it is and move on.

It was a framework I could apply to all kinds of circumstances, and after a while it would become second nature to me and I'd begin to think positively in an instinctive way. Given how ingrained those negative thoughts were, and how loud the chatterbox seemed to me, I couldn't imagine how long this would take. One thing was certain, there was no way to wave a magic wand and wake up cured: it was up to me to knuckle down and brave it out.

When I did this, it showed me just how much my parents had influenced me. I'd thought that just by cutting them out of my life I would be free of them, but now I understood that I was still carrying them around with me. They were there in the chatterbox, chipping away at my self-esteem and twisting my thoughts. I allowed the things they had done years ago to keep me chained, and worse still, I was doing their work for them, dragging myself into their cycle of pessimism and anger – the opposite to what I wanted for myself.

In effect, they were still in control of me, because I let them be. Walking out hadn't been enough to empower me; I wasn't winning, and the little girl I had been was still trapped and confused.

CHAPTER 26

Glimmers of hope

While I was staying in hospital, listening to other residents and mulling over what came up in my therapy sessions, I started to make my peace with that little girl. I saw what had been done to her by my father and mother, and I also realised why she had acted the way she did. The greatest thing I learned was that it had not been her fault. That was how I began to let go of the nightmares that tormented her and me, and began to lead us out of the dark maze we were lost in.

We didn't deserve to be punished or blamed for all those cruelties — whatever my parents told me about how useless and horrible I was, it didn't mean that I had to believe them. My life could be worth something, and I owed that to the little girl too. We had to take our worst suffering and turn it into something positive — a lesson, a chance to avoid the mistakes my parents made. A chance to break out of the cycle. Only I could decide what life had in store for me. No-one else could, not then, not now and not ever.

It hadn't all been bleak so far, there was good in my life, and I had had things to be thankful for, too. Those small mercies would be the building blocks for my new, honest life. People had loved me and still did and I had to trust their faith in me. Mandy and Geoff must have seen something in me that was worth their love or they would never have taken me in and done their best to help me. Here were Dan, Lesley and David, still happy to see me, bringing me gifts, unquestioning support and loyalty.

I had to have faith in myself because they had faith in me; Geoff had already got me through the toughest days and he would be with me for as long as I needed him. I knew he'd be watching over me. He'd be there to see me recover the determination I'd once had as a child and forge my new life.

One of the worst things I had to face if I was going to begin that new life with a clean slate was the question of my relationship with Dan. He had been incredible to me, despite what I had done to him. We *had* had good times together, and I adored his family too, but I felt tremendously guilty the more I thought about everything that we had been through.

The thing was, now that I had more insight I knew that even before that horrendous night I had known that I didn't love Dan the way I should if our relationship was going to be for keeps. I had clung on because I was scared of being alone and because I knew I was "incomplete"; I had genuinely believed that I'd be better off in an unhappy relationship than alone.

Now, stone cold vulnerable, I knew that we had to split up once and for all. I couldn't do that as soon as I was aware of it, or even after I'd left hospital, but it was something I worked towards breaking to him as I got stronger.

A lot of the lessons I learned from those therapy sessions didn't come to me till long after I'd left the psychologist's office or even the hospital. I'd go in with questions to ask about what was going on, but never find the right time to ask them, or else the discussion would head off in another direction, and I'd forget. This was a blessing in disguise, because it meant I spent long hours puzzling over things alone, and I discovered the answers for myself. I think that made those lessons all the more influential for me.

I've never ceased to be amazed by the way a therapist can sit with a patient for hours at a time, week in and week out, and do their job so well. Both my psychologist at the hospital and Stephanie had to deal with so much pain and high emotion. The rewards of their work are hard fought for, but every success is a life saved. Without their gentle suggestions and endless patience, I would *never* have found my way out of that hell.

After a week or so I noticed that things were picking up. I could see that I'd made progress when I saw the manner in which the new in-patients acted on their first night. I knew what stage they were at, and knew I'd passed it, and that meant I was getting better. My psychologist told me that when I did check out, I must come back as a day patient and continue to receive all the same therapies. I'd pictured myself leaving and having to pick up the pieces of my life where I'd left them, and knowing that my treatment would continue was a massive relief.

Jolts of happiness were beginning to hit me. I'd made some new friends and we'd all go and sit outside in the garden with our coffee and our fags and chat away like we'd known each other for years. Each night the staff circulated a chart with a list of the next day's menu on it, and we had to choose what we wanted to eat. For fun I'd tick extra boxes for people, so they'd end up with a plate of pilchards as well as the food they'd been expecting. They'd be baffled, and the nurses would swear blind they'd ordered it, and my friends and I would be at the other end of the table laughing till we cried. It did no harm and started our day on a high.

One thing I talked about with both my friends and my psychologist was changing my surname. My father's family name was distinctive, and his notoriety had ensured that plenty of people in my home town only had to hear it for them to make all kinds of assumptions about me too. I didn't want to be tarred with the same brush and was convinced it was holding me back in my career and life.

Choosing a new name would disassociate me once and for all from my father and mark my re-birth as the person I hoped to become. I'd told my friends that I wanted to write a book about everything that had happened so that it would help people who'd been in the same circumstances and, encouraged by my progress, they promised to look out for it. We'd spend hours flicking through magazines and books to try and find a suitable name, but nothing was coming up. I had a feeling I'd know it when I heard it.

One evening when we were sitting round in front of the television, a trailer for a famous film came on. I remembered seeing it years ago. The actress who starred in it was one that I'd admired for years for her brave, no-messing persona. I said her name in my head, then tried out my name with her surname, and it all fell into place. I had my new name. I told everyone straightaway: "I've got it! I'm going to be Samantha Weaver, after Sigourney." They all loved it, and thought it sounded perfect, and from that moment on, that's who I was. Samantha Weaver.

I'd been at the hospital for about three weeks when my psychologist suggested I try going home for an evening. Dan came to pick me up and drove me back; it felt odd to be there after so much had happened in the hospital, but I was thrilled to see Boe. While he made us some coffee, Dan suggested that I listen to my answer phone messages. He'd saved some nice ones for me.

What he didn't know was that the first message I got was from Jocelyn. It was bizarre to hear her after all this time, "Sam ... It's Jocelyn. You should know that Dad's had a heart attack. He's in hospital, having a triple heart bypass and he might not pull through." Then she gave the name of the hospital and ward. I put the receiver down in shock. Dan took one look at me and asked me what was wrong. I told him to listen to the message.

I watched his face change from puzzled concern to horror, "Are you ok?" he asked me. I couldn't say much; my immediate thought was that it would be better for everyone if Dad died. There was no way around it; that was the only way to stop him hurting anyone any more. I nodded to Dan and said, "I don't really know what to think." Inside I was just saying to myself, this is typical of the setbacks I've been dished all my life … Nothing ever runs the way I plan it to.

He asked if I wanted to phone the ward or anything like that, and I told him to just give me time to think things through. People had always told me that the bond of blood must mean more to me, and that I couldn't really want my father dead, but they don't know what I saw my family go through at his hands. It's not as if they can possibly appreciate what he did to us all. This time I didn't feel guilty about not giving a damn what happened to him, because I had had an 'inner confirmation' that it was what I truly did feel and no-one could make me question if it was real anymore.

The next day my psychologist made me phone Jocelyn to find out what had happened to Dad. I had been wracking my brains trying to think of whether there was anything I would want to say to him or ask him before he died, and nothing came up. Nothing he could say would give me back my childhood or undo those years of suffering after I left home. I didn't want to call Jocelyn but I did to satisfy my doctor.

Unfortunately my sister confirmed to me that he had made it through the night and was alive, and if I was honest, I was gutted, but also semi-pleased that no-one had been to see him in hospital apart from my mum. It was a type of confirmation that my siblings' feelings ran in parallel with mine even if we were distanced from one another now. My psychologist thought it was lucky in a way that this had happened when I was still a patient, so that we could work through it. "How would you feel if your mother and father died tomorrow? Would you have any regrets?" she asked.

I looked her square in the eyes and said, "No. Much as this may be hard for you to understand, I would actually be relieved. It'd make a lot of things much simpler. If I could go and spit on his grave, I would; he deserves to rot in hell and I hope he does." Annoyingly, I could see she didn't really believe me. She was waiting for me to admit that maybe I cared what happened to him after all, but I now honestly knew that just wasn't the case.

With my paranoia biting at my ankles I retaliated to her sceptical look; "I'm sick and tired of people doubting me when I say that," I continued sternly, "I do mean it." She nodded and smiled, "Because they don't understand what happened to you. It's impossible for them to do that." That last comment softened me – not towards my dad, but to others. I had to become more tolerant of other people's reactions and not expect them to grasp the situation so well. Just because they did disagree, it didn't mean I had to change the way I thought. I'd have to learn to leave it at that instead of fighting and getting resentful or even justifying myself!

As it drew towards the end of my time as an in-patient, I collected my thoughts and made myself face what was waiting for me in the "outside world". A lot of effort − well, I knew that already. Explaining to people where I'd been for a few months − this I didn't care about so much any more. I didn't want to become fixated on what others' opinions were and torture myself with obsessions beyond my control. I know I'm not crazy, and I don't have to accept the judgement of anyone who says I am; besides, everyone might actually be very sympathetic, despite what I was expecting. The fact was that I had been depressed and I'd tried everything I could to get well, but I'd needed some extra help and there is nothing wrong in that and, I'd decided, nothing to be ashamed of. The hospital had given me that. A break, and a new direction.

There was the ominous knowledge that my parents still lived in the same town as me, and that they could see what car I was driving or what clothes I was wearing − all kinds of details of my life. My psychologist said I should consider moving if they were too close for comfort, but my feelings were mixed. After all, that flat had been the first place I could call my own, and I didn't see why that security should be taken away from me − yet again − by my family. I'd have to ponder that one a bit longer.

At least I knew I could walk through my local streets and hold my head up high in the knowledge that I hadn't gone out of my way to do anything wrong to anyone. My parents might think they can do that too, but they know deep down that they should hang their heads in shame. They might put on their nicest manners and pretend to be lovely people, but I know different.

CHAPTER 27

Small steps

The day I left, my psychologist congratulated me for doing so well, and I felt a swell of long-forgotten pride. My chatterbox also kicked in to imply that the staff said that to everyone to bolster their self-esteem, but that just reminded me that I still had a long way to go. My future started there.

I didn't want to feel overwhelmed by all I had to do on leaving hospital. The best way to organise my thoughts was to set goals for myself. To think about what would happen a week down the line was too far away for me, I had to take things inch by inch to avoid getting exhausted and depressed. I had to tackle my relationship with Dan, but not just yet.

Instead, every morning I would make plans for what I would achieve in the afternoon, and by the end of the afternoon I'd work out what I had to do in the evening. I found this gave me structure and took the pressure off. These small steps allowed me to change my mind or adapt my plans if I felt too tired to deal with them.

My first goal was to officially change my name, and I did that via the Internet. After entering my details I sent off my birth certificate and within a few weeks I officially became Samantha Weaver. Mandy was my witness.

I went back to work part-time with the good grace of my ever-patient boss Louise, who did her best to see that I eased back into my job as gently as possible. I began to make plans for whole days at a time, although sometimes I gave myself a break and went back to thinking about things by mornings and afternoons. I had learned not to see this as some kind of relapse, but accepted the need to do it and moved on. I still work this way, by making mini goals and reaching them, and I found I grew in confidence.

I started to say "no" to things I would have previously felt obliged to say "yes" to, and I said "yes" to things I would have turned down in the past. I worked at not seeing the worst possible scenario in everything I was offered, and I found myself discovering all kinds of new things. Since I'd been little I'd always wanted a horse, but of course I knew we could never afford one. When I left hospital I booked myself riding lessons which I adored.

I kept up the yoga and started listening to the music I liked, rather than stuff that I'd thought was more "socially acceptable". Now I wouldn't let myself fester at home doing nothing, but made myself call a friend and go out. When I chatted with people I didn't feel as though I had to agree with them all the time, or, as used to happen to me, end up arguing a point passionately. We could agree to differ.

Once I'd started my new hobbies I found it easier to talk with people too, because I had something to support who I was and what I liked. At first nothing flowed naturally and I felt awkward talking about my new loves, but over time the nagging idea that they were bored with me, or thought I was wrong, began to dissipate. Little things bothered me less.

I addressed one aspect of myself that needed improving at a time. If I was unhappy with something I had said or done I'd try to work out why I'd behaved like that and if I was being too sensitive. I've never been a laidback person and it certainly wasn't easy for me to try and keep a rein on my emotions when something bothered me. I still slip up from time to time.

One thing I did was to spend more time with people who were very easy going and see how they dealt with the same situations. Clearly they knew that there was no point in behaving irrationally and blowing things out of all proportion. I took a leaf out of their books and endeavoured not to get worked up if there was nothing I could do about something.

One day I accidentally clipped a colleague's car when I was parking at work and scratched the paintwork. I was prepared to pay for the damage rather than make an insurance claim, but she was adamant that that was just what she wanted to do. I tried to explain that it would affect my insurance premium and that it would make no difference to her – either way, she wouldn't have to pay for the work, but she got irate and started shouting and swearing at me.

I backed out of the debate before I could get defensive and let things escalate, but later discovered that she'd been complaining to other colleagues about it behind my back. I went back to ask her why she had such a problem, and she laid into me again, and I found myself answering back and before I knew it we were in the middle of a big row. Eventually it sorted itself out, but it was another lesson learned the hard way for me.

If the same thing happened now I'd take a deep breath, try to relax my shoulders and think about something else. Then I wouldn't lock horns with the person; I can't make someone do something if they don't want to, especially if reasoning with them calmly has failed. The best thing is just to drop it and move on, and maybe have a little moan about it to someone neutral.

I do have to accept that I'm a highly strung person and I won't always win that battle, but it doesn't mean I should hate myself. It just means I have to keep on working at it. On the whole it's working and I'm less irritable now that I've learned a degree of tolerance.

I'm still doing battle with my anxiety, and so far my victories there are small. It's not easy because I've been scared of so many things, and have difficulty coping with anything unfamiliar to me. When I feel the first stirring of anxiety about a trip into new territory I always try and ask myself what's the worst that could happen. On occasion it works and the feeling of being in control of my anxiety makes me feel totally empowered. Other times it fails, and I have to try a different approach.

I've always got very wound up at the thought of travelling on my own by train and I've got no idea why that, of all things, should bother me. I worry about getting the wrong platform or getting on a different train or missing my station – stupid things. I decided to face the fear by booking myself a train trip to see a friend in Newcastle on my own, changing at Birmingham on the way.

I got on the train with a bit of back up from Dan, but I was so busy chatting to someone as a way of calming my nerves that we were pulling out of Birmingham before I noticed. Immediately I felt my throat tighten and my breathing shift. I went straight into my relaxation exercises, telling myself that it would be OK and I should wait for a ticket inspector and ask him what I could do.

After what seemed like hours but was probably only minutes, one appeared and informed me that the train didn't stop till Manchester, though he promised me I could catch a connecting train to Newcastle from there. By that point I was in a state of barely suppressed panic and thought I might break down and lose it in front of everyone. I was in such a terrible way that I spent a fortune on a taxi to get me there instead, feeling equal parts stupid and hysterical.

It may be a while before I can make another go of it. Because of that illogical fear I've missed out on training programmes for work, nights out with friends, trips to see people – all things I would have loved. I'm getting there, but I'm taking it more slowly now, travelling with a couple of people and working out how the train system works. More recently I travelled into London and back alone. There was a problem part way, but I got it sorted and am proud of myself for achieving that. Maybe next time I might try the underground once I'm there instead of taking a taxi. Small steps.

The hardest habit to break is my defensiveness. I spent years trying to protect myself from being hurt by getting in the first blow and I know it had made me a very prickly person. It felt like I had an antenna constantly buzzing above my head and letting off an alarm bell at the smallest sign of trouble. Often it was something I'd just imagined, but by then it was too late and I was in self-protection mode.

I'd jump into a conversation and talk over what someone else was saying to try and have my say before they could criticise me, and it must have looked very aggressive. If a colleague started talking about something that had gone wrong at work I'd interrupt with a battery of reasons why it wasn't my fault and that could aggravate people no end. It landed me in a lot of unnecessary arguments.

When the alarm bell goes off I have to try and calm myself and let the other person have their say so I could work out exactly what the problem was. The effect is dramatic; instead of both of us tensing and raising our voices, we can talk in a civilised way and the issue is resolved. I go away feeling satisfied and safe in the knowledge that I've managed it once, at least. Once becomes twice, then three times and soon I've succeeded in staying off the defensive more times than I've messed it up. That gives me the drive to keep going because I know eventually I'll come out on top of my emotions.

In the past I'd been my own harshest critic, and my new method of monitoring my thoughts and feelings didn't mean that I'd become more judgemental about myself. If anything, it meant the opposite. I used to set myself goals that were unrealistic and then attack myself for not reaching them. Happiness had been measured out in material things – house, car, promotion, holidays – and not what it really was. That just threw me into a vicious cycle of more ridiculous goals, more self-hate and more depression. I'd set myself up for disappointment.

What I now did was to write these "failures" off as one big learning curve and it made them a source of experience, not regret. You can't evolve as a person if you don't try new things and risk getting them wrong sometimes. After all, who knows where I'd be stuck if I hadn't screwed up the courage to take that first step towards help? You can turn a disaster into a valuable lesson that will give you new opportunities in the long run.

When I'd been home for a couple of months I felt stable enough to face up to what was going on in my relationship with Dan. I'd been unable to shake the sense that he'd been disappointed that there wasn't a huge difference in me, and at the same time I felt that he was holding me back with his memories of how things had been before I broke down. I can understand how it must have been very tough for him to have me back again, but I knew I was the only one who could understand the gradual changes I'd managed to make to my outlook.

I believed it was the kindest thing to do for both our sakes if I ended things and protected him from further heartache. In the end it was a mutual separation and it was very hard. He had been a rock and I certainly wasn't well yet; I was willingly leaving myself vulnerable but I knew I had to do it. Alone I had more space to think over all the questions that hospital had left me with, and I was the only person who had the answers.

We've spoken since and remain committed friends. His friendship means so very much to me. We can talk about what happened and have each dealt with it in our own way. He went through more with me than any of my other boyfriends and stuck with me in awful times when I felt barely human anymore. I selfishly expected him to understand, and he gave me more encouragement than I could have hoped for. His parents never wavered in their support either and I can never thank them enough for that.

I've stayed on good terms with a handful of the others too and I couldn't have better friends. They say that all they want is to see me happy and they've never held a grudge despite having seen me be difficult and hurtful. My self-destructiveness affected them too, something I wasn't aware of at the time. My doctor once pointed out the pattern in my relationships, and how I'd reach a certain point at two or two and a half years in, then begin to sabotage things. I'd get bored and resentful and "test" my boyfriends' love for me. That was a direct result of my depression and defensiveness.

I didn't have the self-esteem to think anyone could love me, and I honestly believed they were only there because they felt sorry for me. I kept comparing myself to their exes and obsessed about whether they were more beautiful or better lovers. Whatever my boyfriends assured me – that I was pretty, or funny, or nice, it was never enough to satisfy my craving for reassurance. The person I really needed the reassurance from was myself, but I just couldn't see it at the time.

Even if I'm in a relationship I have to be able to stand alone and not rely on other people. I used to depend on others to pick me up or tell me I was behaving badly; I watched them for clues about how to do what I thought were the right, "socially acceptable" things. I just asked them if I was doing things correctly rather than trusting my own gut instinct, and that was because I had no belief in myself. Now I tried to listen to my inner voice and decide for myself.

With time I began to feel less alone. The black hole was shrinking. I still relied on Geoff being there for me and knew he'd be the constant in my life, providing comfort when I was in tears and answers when I'd tried everything and drawn a blank. I still have that promise to keep, too; there is no way I'm going to let him down now.

I began to smile and mean it; the warm feelings I'd never expected to experience again came back to me bit by bit. I felt excitement for the first time since I was a child. I had started to heal and become myself. I had no other way to turn, but now I had a safety net that I'd created for myself, and I could step out towards that better life without fear, and that was thrilling. I was going to get mad, cast down, angry and frustrated, but that was just part of the journey, and I would know happiness too.

I could finally leave my parents' voices behind me and move out of the shadows that had jailed me. There would be no more waiting for comfort, I had myself and my future, which seemed lit up. I'd picked myself up and brushed myself off and now that I knew I'd done it once, I could certainly do it again if times ever got tough again. I'd been reborn without even realising it, and I shone as brightly as the North Star.

I've put together in my mind a portrait of the person that I want to be, and I'm still striving towards her:

This person would resemble every good thing that I might have to offer
This person would be polite and non-defensive when faced with criticism
This person would be honest when facing dishonesty
This person would be content when feeling insecurity
This person would be strong when facing doubt
This person would be loving when facing hate
This person would be brave when facing fear.

AFTER WORD

I never intended to see my story in print — it was
sort of a joke I had with my fellow patients in hospital.
The writing was originally a therapeutic way of expressing
myself, my hopes, memories and fears during my years of
counselling. When I first started seeing Stephanie I
couldn't think straight because so many questions and
recollections were racing through my mind, and getting
them on to paper was a necessary discipline for me.

At first it all came out in a rush, but later I ran out of
memories and got stuck. I tried to fill in the gaps which
would explain to me why everything had happened, but
both my counsellor and I knew it wasn't working. It
wasn't until I was in hospital and began to keep a diary
that I grew to understand what those explanations were
and how I could move on.

When I left I decided to carry on writing *Saving
Samantha* because a friend who'd read an earlier draft
told me it could be an inspiration to others in the same
situation if I told my story. I'd read a lot of accounts of
child abuse and depression by people like Dave Pelzer,
Kevin Lewis and Julie Gregory but, while their stories

were extraordinary and moving, none of them told me what they'd done to recover from their traumas.

That's why I went ahead with the book, and have made so many private things public. In order to understand how I got better, it was essential to show what had caused me to become so ill in the first place. If you don't approve of what I have laid out here, I don't think you've understood why I wrote this book in the first place. Not for "attention" or kudos, but to try to inspire people to reach out for help and pull themselves out of the black hole of depression.

Depression is a disease that affects most people at some point in their lives, and can turn into a chronic problem. It can be reactive, in response to a traumatic life event like the death of a loved one or financial problems, or it can have a genetic basis. Some sufferers are prone to unrealistic thought processes that cause them to "fail" continuously and blame themselves.

To me depression meant the sensation that I was abnormal and I had always known from a very young age that there was something not quite right about me. I was isolated and confused and when I couldn't put those feelings into perspective I got paranoid and angry.

The best thing that happened was that I realised I needed help from a professional. This took great courage because I had the stereotyped ideas of mental health care that a lot of people imagine to be the reality. It wasn't like that, of course, and there were many options for treatment for me to choose, from medication to counselling and therapies.

I consider myself fortunate to have had a superb GP who was always kind and never patronising. She never tried to force me to do anything, and made sure I understood what was going on as best I could in my muddled state. I know not everyone has that sort of back up from their family practitioner.

Depressed people are not necessarily insane, although that's what I believed because I thought my father was mad. I've questioned my own levels of sanity so many times I can't count them, but I'm 99.9% certain that I am sane and the difference between the two states is now clear in my mind. Depression makes you sad, not mad.

There are certain triggers that can push a person from depression into suicidal thinking, and recognising those is essential if you are to catch yourself before you give in to the urge to harm yourself. Maybe you've become very reliant on someone but that relationship has broken down, or you've noticed that the people around you seem to think you're over-reacting to events. Perhaps you've become very withdrawn and are no longer acting like your old self.

There's no class or type of person who is exempt from it – not children, the elderly, builders, doctors, therapists! In fact doctors represent a fair percentage of "successful suicides" recorded every year. From those statistics it's possible to see that the only factor that regularly lowers the suicide risk is strong spiritual or religious convictions.

The so-called "death fantasy" is a powerful and seductive one. I should know, I experienced it often enough. I'd think through different ways of killing myself and dismiss any that I might survive – if I took pills they could pump my stomach, for example, or if I ran in front of a car I might end up in a coma and pull through. Dying looks like the best escape from the unbearable pain you're undergoing. Even when I was a child I thought that, and on a few occasions held my breath until I passed out just to see what would happen. The feeling I got before I fainted was bizarrely soothing.

I believe to this day that one of the reasons I initially turned to suicide attempts was because of my father's example. Influenced as I was by my parents, it seemed to me like a "normal" way to respond to trauma and confusion or to make a cry for help, rather than dealing with what was happening. I thought as a child that if I threatened to harm myself the Social Services or the police would get involved and rescue me, but it didn't work out that way. After years of threatening myself and those close to me with killing myself, it simply became a habit.

I also began to imagine my own funeral and what people would say when they finally realised how terrible things had been for me. Of course, the death fantasy obscures the fact that if you had told people your fears instead, they could understand and help you. When I thought about my funeral I couldn't imagine anyone turning up because I hated myself so much, and that obviously only made things worse.

A death fantasy can turn into your automatic response to stress or crises and it lulls you into thinking of death as a friendly escape. In reality, you can escape depression when you are alive, and I hope I'm proof of that. It's also the case that every suicide leaves a trail of devastated friends and family behind them, causing great misery and only passing on the depression to others.

Why do so many people get so ill undetected and take this drastic final step? Depression is still a taboo subject. There may be lots of accounts of it published, but when it comes down to talking honestly person to person about the disease, we still avoid the issue. If you're a sufferer you think people will judge you as being "weak" if you admit that you are suicidal, when in reality it takes a great deal of determination to carry out that threat. We're afraid too, of not being understood. It all boils down to a fear of the unknown – sufferers don't know what reaction they'll get if they confess. Those who are outside that are afraid of the idea of death itself and the seriousness of the illness, and instead of trying to understand it they categorise it in the way that society does, as "a mental illness, a madness which needs addressing".

Depressives are not always easy to get along with and can just seem awkward or selfish, but you have to see where that behaviour might stem from. I hope that by giving my whole life story here I can also help people who have no personal experience of depression to see what might be causing a friend, relative or colleague to act so strangely. It can be difficult to be sympathetic if someone isn't open with you about their real, underlying feelings, but you must see that they are held back by their own fear, shame and the taboo.

There are many things that we don't think we can discuss but which could be defeated if we were able to talk openly about them. "Abuse" is one. It's a dramatic word, but it barely begins to cover what it actually means to an individual. To abuse is to mistreat, and while I worry about some of the connotations associated with the word nowadays I have to use it because I was mistreated as a child.

How anyone could defend themselves by saying that their victim deserved abuse I will never know. No-one has that right. I think that only those who enjoy the feeling of control and power that this behaviour gives them can be said to be abusers. They are also the ones who continue to dish out the same treatment, over and over again.

I feel very strongly that an abuser is more than aware of what they are doing, and that they cannot pass the blame for all their cruelties on to someone else. They have to face the consequences of their actions instead, and stop the chain there.

My father was a monster who exploited his position as an adult to put my family through terrible things. He blamed his own parents, but now I see that is no excuse. As someone who has endured abuse I can safely say that I would never put another living soul through the hell I underwent.

I know parents are not given a guide book on how to raise a happy child and most try their hardest to do what they think is best, but the reality is there are many out there who take advantage of their position of power. They don't consider the detrimental effects that this will have on a child or how difficult it will be to undo it. Perhaps they simply don't care?

We expect parents to know right from wrong and teach their children that, but people like my parents just scare their sons and daughters into submission and they grow up into difficult, wary adults who have been stripped of a normal range of emotions. I still find myself wondering, if I'd been given the nurturing love and support that I've seen others receive from their families, I might have turned out differently. What could I have achieved if I hadn't been contaminated by that constant fear? The only difference now is that I do not dwell on it constantly, allowing it to blight my progress because I know it will serve no purpose.

I also think about where I'd be if I hadn't cut myself off from everyone. My instinct tells me I wouldn't have survived. The dysfunctional way they were living, their standards and morals, may have been ok for them, but not for me. I couldn't have kept in touch with them if it meant condoning their behaviour – and I don't.

I still dislike them, but not with the overwhelming passion I used to know. I shan't re-establish contact, but I'm safe in the knowledge that I've dealt with my issues and moved on. They no longer hold me back or influence my present or my future.

My chatterbox is with me even now, but it's not the same presence it once was in my mind. When it rears its ugly head I can ignore it or double check myself and work out why I'm experiencing it again – did something recent trigger an old memory of something traumatic? Am I just tired? I'll never let it beat me, though.

I admit the tactic of constantly re-examining my emotions and reactions is tiresome, but as time goes on I need to do it less and less. We're forever evolving as individuals and we can turn that to our advantage by building our experience and transforming negative thought cycles into positive.

Since leaving hospital I've come to realise that we all have a purpose in life. I have lived through more in 26 years than a lot of people would ever experience in life. It has made me a stronger person and given me the courage I need in order to succeed in life according to my own standards. What doesn't kill us only makes us stronger.

I am not in the least religious, but I do take comfort in Karma. If others choose to take comfort in faith or religion and it works for them, then great, who is anyone to knock it? At the end of the day, we all have something that we fall back on. Our paths are mapped out and we each experience life differently for a reason. Everyone has their own limits, one person may be able to deal with something well, in comparison to another, and that is what makes us unique. If we all had the ability to do the same things then there would be no such thing as resolution, compromise, understanding … the list is endless. No-one would be unique, and what a boring world that would be.

I would not wish the life and experiences I have endured on anyone. I can look back now and put what I have learned to good use. I've armed myself with the ability to cope in more or less every situation; I now have a real hope that things will get better. I can still remember the time that I didn't have hope and I don't ever want to feel that way again. It's not possible to go through tough times and hurtful experiences and come out of it unscathed, but you can fix the damage that's been done.

If this book makes a difference to one person, it will have done its job. I hope that it will encourage these people to do what they need to in order to live a happy, content and fulfilled life. There is help out there, it isn't always easy to find, but if you want it badly enough, you will find it and if you want to get better, you will get there one day. It is not an easy road to recovery – you have to get worse before you can get better – but with the right support and the right attitude I am positive many more people will get there in the end. When suffering with depression, reaching a point where you can see some positive things for yourself is nothing short of a massive achievement, and you have to take great pride in that.

I have finally come to the end of my journey; I have a smile on my face, feelings of well-being, happiness and excitement inside me. The prospect of tomorrow no longer fills me with dread. But most importantly I hope and believe that things will improve for me now that I am confident I will be able to cope with whatever life throws my way. I have a future; something I never thought would be mine until now. As one chapter closes in my life I look forward to a new chapter beginning. I have a solid and firm belief that I've got something good to look forward to now and with that in mind … I plan to live my life.

ABOUT THE AUTHOR

Samantha C. Weaver has first-hand knowledge of what it is like to suffer from anxiety, severe clinical depression and related stress, and she knows how hard it can be to recover from this debilitating illness. She is not embarrassed or ashamed to talk about her experiences and has become a national spokesperson on behalf of depression sufferers everywhere. She is featured on the award winning charity website DIPEx *(Database of Individual Patient Experiences)* and has been interviewed by numerous international papers and magazines talking about her personal experiences of living with, coping with and overcoming depression.

Samantha has written several articles on depression as an expert author at Ezine Articles and is currently working on her second book, a self-help guide for depression sufferers. She is a member of the Society of Authors and the Author's Licensing and Collective Society (ALCS) and owner of the Authors & Writers Forum. She is also working toward her diploma in counselling via distance learning with the Institute of Counselling.

After years of suffering from this illness, Samantha reluctantly admitted herself into a private psychiatric hospital, and after months of intense treatment and much personal reflection, she has learned how to help herself. Now fully recovered, it is her mission in life to help people do what she has done … find complete and total recovery.

For more information visit Samantha's website at http://www.samanthaweaver.com

We hope you enjoyed this Hay House book.
If you would like to receive a free catalogue featuring additional
Hay House books and products, or if you would like information
about the Hay Foundation, please contact:

Hay House UK Ltd
Unit B • 292 Kensal Road • London W10 5BE
Tel: (44) 20 8962 1230; Fax: (44) 20 8962 1239
www.hayhouse.co.uk
****

Published and distributed in the United States of America by:
Hay House, Inc. • P.O. Box 5100 • Carlsbad, CA 92018-5100
Tel: (1) 760 431 7695 or (800) 654 5126; Fax: (1) 760 431 6948 or (800) 650 5115
www.hayhouse.com
****

Published and distributed in Australia by:
Hay House Australia Ltd • 18/36 Ralph St • Alexandria NSW 2015
Tel: (61) 2 9669 4299 • Fax: (61) 2 9669 4144
www.hayhouse.com.au
****

Published and distributed in the Republic of South Africa by:
Hay House SA (Pty) Ltd • PO Box 990 • Witkoppen 2068
Tel/Fax: (27) 11 706 6612 • orders@psdprom.co.za
****

Distributed in Canada by:
Raincoast • 9050 Shaughnessy St • Vancouver, BC V6P 6E5
Tel: (1) 604 323 7100 • Fax: (1) 604 323 2600
****

Sign up via the Hay House UK website to receive the Hay House
online newsletter and stay informed about what's going on with
your favourite authors. You'll receive bimonthly announcements
about discounts and offers, special events, product highlights,
free excerpts, giveaways, and more!

www.hayhouse.co.uk